Disciplined Hope

Disciplined Hope

Prayer, Politics, and Resistance

by
Shannon Craigo-Snell

CASCADE Books • Eugene, Oregon

DISCIPLINED HOPE
Prayer, Politics, and Resistance

Copyright © 2019 Shannon Craigo-Snell. All rights reserved. Except for brief quotations in critical publications or reviews, no part of this book may be reproduced in any manner without prior written permission from the publisher. Write: Permissions, Wipf and Stock Publishers, 199 W. 8th Ave., Suite 3, Eugene, OR 97401.

Cascade Books
An Imprint of Wipf and Stock Publishers
199 W. 8th Ave., Suite 3
Eugene, OR 97401

www.wipfandstock.com

PAPERBACK ISBN: 978-1-5326-4552-5
HARDCOVER ISBN: 978-1-5326-4553-2
EBOOK ISBN: 978-1-5326-4554-9

Cataloguing-in-Publication data:

Names: Craigo-Snell, Shannon Nichole.

Title: Disciplined hope : prayer, politics, and resistance / Shannon Craigo-Snell.

Description: Eugene, OR : Cascade Books, 2019 | Includes bibliographical references.

Identifiers: ISBN 978-1-5326-4552-5 (paperback) | ISBN 978-1-5326-4553-2 (hardcover) | ISBN 978-1-5326-4554-9 (ebook)

Subjects: LCSH: Christianity and politics. | Christianity and justice. | Prayers.

Classification: BR115.P7 C73 2019 (paperback) | BR115.P7 C73 (ebook)

Manufactured in the U.S.A.   01/14/19

To Oshel and Joanna Craigo
who taught me to read voraciously, to follow politics,
and to work for the common good.

Contents

Preface • ix
Acknowledgments • xi
Introduction • 1
Prayers • 19
Bibliography • 131

Preface

This book reflects on an experiment with prayers posted on Facebook during the first year of the Trump administration, prayers that lifted up the work of people and groups who were resisting hatred and working for the common good. Given all that has unfolded regarding the role of Facebook during the 2016 election—Russian bots spreading political discord and lies, ads purchased to disrupt democracy, and the sale of massive amounts of user information—the content of the prayers and the tool of their delivery are at odds. I note the irony.

Readers of these prayers will note that they draw daily from the work of journalists. The bibliography recognizes reporters from many reliable news sources, from a high school paper to local newspapers in various cities to national and international papers. This book is, in a very real way, a love letter to the reporters, investigators, fact-checkers, authors, and editors who make democracy possible through the free press.

Acknowledgments

I am grateful for the efforts of many who have contributed to this text and supported this project. Megan McCarty read over prayers for me all year and helped compile the references. Joanna Hipp offered prayer suggestions, gave feedback on the introduction, and, most graciously, took over the practice of daily prayer. I give thanks to all who drew my attention to those for whom we could intercede and to all who joined this experimental community of prayer.

Tom Zoellner, Danielle Tumminio, and Shawnthea Monroe offered comments that greatly improved the introduction. In addition to the incredible support he normally provides for my work, Seth Craigo-Snell also gave excellent editorial advice and performed bibliographic miracles.

Introduction

This is an account of an experiment, during a time of political chaos, in the first year Donald Trump held the office of President of the United States. It offers a record of prayerful resistance in a time of regular outrages. It also offers a theology of prayer as a political act.

The Experiment

On the morning of November 9, 2016, I was in a state of confusion and panic. Confusion that the people of the United States had—with all appropriate caveats about popular vote versus electoral college—elected a person who was openly sexist, racist, dishonest, and completely unqualified for the office of the presidency. And yet, millions of Americans voted for him.

As a professor who studies issues of social justice, I considered myself clear-sighted and realistic about the United States. But I was most unsettled by the exit polls that revealed the majority of white, female voters chose Trump. As a white, middle-aged, Christian woman, I felt betrayed and displaced. In public settings near where I live in Kentucky, I began to view anyone who looked like me with suspicion. The "we" that I was part of by virtue of being a white woman had proven itself to be harmful to the "we" of my loves and commitments.

The rhetoric of the incoming administration did not threaten me directly. However, everyone I love and the common world we inhabit seemed radically vulnerable: friends and family members of different races, religions, sexual orientations, and gender identities. Looming over all of this was dire concern for our environment. In the face of international consensus on the facts of climate change, the incoming administration promised to abdicate responsibility and roll back regulations designed to protect the earth.

Disciplined Hope

My panic took me into new territory. In keeping with Gen-X stereotypes, I've never considered myself particularly attached to institutions of any kind. However, after November 2016 I realized there were institutions I took for granted that I value greatly. Institutions like public schools, the social safety net, checks and balances within the democratic process, the rule of law, the free press, and on and on.

After decades of being comfortable as a political lefty, I realized I am invested in *conserving* many institutions, ideals, and aspirations of the United States.

The early days after the election had a steep learning curve. My confusion slowly gave way to recognition that I had been naïve. One day I was walking across campus, looking distressed, when Alexis, an African-American, female student, came up and hugged me tight. She said, "I know you are surprised and you don't know how we are going to survive this. But what is happening now is not something new. Things that have always been wrong with America are being uncovered." She reminded me that God is—and always has been—with us in the struggle for a better world.

Alicia's comment did not allay my fears in that moment, but I suspect it laid the groundwork for the idea that emerged on January 24. I had spent over two weeks prior to that day in a constant state of emotional turmoil and rational recoil at the illogical plans and dishonest words of the incoming administration. I oscillated between anger and fear, outrage and anxiety. This was no way to live. Furthermore, I was convinced it was exactly how the new administration wanted people like myself to feel. No one is more easily manipulated than those who are fearful. Outrage expends a lot of energy, often undirected.

My anxious state was evident in my prayer life. Christian faith involves prayer, which takes many forms. My prayers during that time of turmoil centered on asking God to protect the people, places, and institutions that seemed under attack. In both verbal and non-verbal ways, I poured out my fear, anger, and longing for a better world. Yet even these prayers were monochromatic, in that they responded to perceived danger. I was in a defensive stance in my prayer life. And yet, the Bible says "Do not fear" (Isaiah 41:10). Repeatedly (Isaiah 35:4, 40:9, 41:10, and many others). I needed to do something to force myself out of a fear-based posture, at least a little bit.

I decided that every day, I would lift up a person or group that was actively resisting the fear and hate that dominated our national politics. This was intended as a personal discipline—something that I set out to do

Introduction

for my own benefit. Because disciplines can be difficult to stick to, I decided to post my plan, and my prayers, on Facebook, as a form of communal accountability. So I began, every day, to seek out news stories of people working for the common good and posting a brief prayer for them.

The response was surprising. I received consistent feedback that these small prayers were useful to those who read them. The prayers were helpful reminders of the good efforts underway, tiny rejoinders to the onslaught of bad news. A community began to form. It was geographically, racially, and socio-economically diverse, and it included people with multiple religious backgrounds and spiritual commitments. People began to send me prayer requests, identifying resisters to lift up. For many, it became a daily devotion.

I confess that some days I was sick, or traveling, or too tired from other commitments to post a prayer. By then end of the year, I also found the necessary amount of news reading onerous. I needed to skip a day or two of reading three newspapers to find positive examples. By January 23, 2018, I was grateful to pass the torch of daily prayers for resisters to Rev. Joanna Hipp, a friend and former student.

Each of the prayers was topical, sparked by an event of the day. In this way, they serve as a record of sorts—what happened in the first year of the Trump administration, seen through the lens of how we resisted. More importantly, this year of public, political prayer is an opportunity to reflect on prayer itself.

Theology

Even our most esoteric theological concepts begin with what actual people do in their lives of faith. For example, the doctrine of the Trinity—that God is three in one—developed out of attempts to articulate why early Christians baptized "in the name of the Father, Son, and Holy Spirit." The lived practices of the faithful come first (sometimes called first-order theology) and then theologians reflect on these and articulate something of their meaning (sometimes called second-order theology). Sometimes, theological reflections lead to new insights, questions, or challenges for the community in whose practices they began.

The theology that follows is a reflection on the practices of prayer in the midst of political turmoil. While my own faith is located within the traditions of Christianity, and therefore these are the resources upon which

I draw, the community that prayed together in 2017 included many who live within other religious traditions or do not identify with any religious tradition. It is my hope that this theology of prayer can similarly be of use in expansive contexts.

Prayer as Relating

Prayer takes many forms, including focused contemplation, silent listening for the Holy, participating in political demonstrations, styles of reading sacred texts, ways of dancing and music-making, ritual actions, the communal recitation of traditional prayers in liturgy, and the desperate plea for help. Yet within this diversity there is a common thread of seeking connection with the Holy.

Theologian Marilyn McCord Adams frames all types of prayer in terms of relationship with God, writing, "prayer is simply a way of being in the world with God."[1] The lens of relationship allows McCord Adams to draw analogies between children and parents or romantic partners. We build relationships with one another through "wordless presence," "carnal knowledge," "articulate speech," and "joint activities."[2]

> Being in the world with God person-to-person is just as multifaceted as children's growing up in their parents' home and life partners' sharing a household. Here below, togetherness sometimes takes the form of wordless presence (as with mother and child, or lovers staring into one another's eyes) and carnal knowledge (as with a mother nursing her baby or the lover's invasive and enfolding touch). Other times, the medium of exchange is articulate speech—from greetings and compliments to trading information (what needs to be fetched from the store, which parts of the house or car need repair), from vigorous debates and deliberative conversations and angry quarrels to make-up apologies. Still other times, life together takes the form of joint activities: digging the garden and planting the flowers, raking leaves and cleaning the gutters, hiking in the woods, throwing a party, organizing with others for political action. Life together builds a history of shared memories that constitute the narrative of who we are.[3]

---

1. McCord Adams, "Prayer as the 'Lifeline of Theology,'" 272.
2. McCord Adams, "Prayer as the 'Lifeline of Theology,'" 273.
3. McCord Adams, "Prayer as the 'Lifeline of Theology,'" 273–74.

Introduction

McCord Adams's analogies honor the significance of many different ways of praying. The category of wordless presence has room for meditation, centering prayer, attending to nature, and many other practices. Carnal knowledge makes space for liturgical practices such as the Eucharist, rituals, and the many ways we relate to God in the bodily relations of care, passion, and compassion that we have with other human beings. It could also include the feeling of sun on one's skin or the routine of swimming every morning.

The category of articulate speech might seem more limited, as it does presume a person is speaking directly to God (or the saints, in some traditions). However, it is still expansive. Much corporate prayer—prayers of a whole group together—is articulate speech, such as hymns, prayers written out in the church bulletin, and memorized prayers recited together (such as The Lord's Prayer or The Serenity Prayer). Articulate prayer can also be individual, from saying the Rosary to a child reciting "Now I Lay Me Down to Sleep" at bedtime. All of the articulate prayers I have mentioned so far have been scripted, but of course spoken prayer includes spontaneous words, either in a group or individually. Perhaps the prayers with which we are most familiar are the whispered pleas for help, the gasped words of gratitude when danger passes, or even the desperate deals we try to strike with the Divine. Unlike most of the scripted prayers printed in church bulletins, our spontaneous prayers to God can be angry, demanding, questioning, accusatory, and argumentative. McCord Adams emphasizes that this is part of learning to live with someone, like a parent or a partner, and says that God takes even angry prayers as positive steps towards relationship. God desires relationship with us and welcomes all our efforts. Fran, a prayer-mentor of mine, describes some of her spoken prayers to God in ways that remind me of text messaging with my closest friends. She tells God what is going on in her life, including the important stuff and the minute bits of joy, disappointment, and humor. She talks to God like an old friend.

McCord Adams's final category, shared activities, is particularly relevant to the topic of praying in a time of political strife. In 1965, Rabbi Abraham Joshua Heschel marched with Rev. Dr. Martin Luther King Jr. in Selma, Alabama. Afterwards, he said of marching, "I felt my legs were praying."[4] The phrase "praying with our feet" has been embraced by many politically active people who understand their efforts at creating a better society—particularly through political change—to be a form of prayer.

4. Heschel, "Their Feet Were Praying."

McCord Adams's category of shared activities conveys this sensibility, that those who work for the common good, for the well-being of their community, for justice and kindness, are engaged in an activity in which God is also involved.

As any parent or partner knows, being in close relationship with another person is hard. It ideally involves all four forms of togetherness. Likewise, McCord Adams's analogies imply that prayer works best when it involves a variety of practices—silent, felt, spoken, and physically enacted.

Of course, these analogies are imperfect, for God is neither a human parent nor a human spouse. God does not, in my experience, change diapers or unload the dishwasher. God is not so neatly contained nor so reliably recognizable. McCord Adams is convinced that God is personal, but this does not mean that God is a big human being in the sky. God exceeds all our human categories and comprehension. This leads to a general rule among Christian theologians, going back to Augustine: if anyone is confident that they completely understand God, then they are not talking about God at all.

God is not obvious, is mysterious, is portrayed in multiple and competing ways. The hard evidence around us does not easily lead to the conclusion that we are in relationship with the Holy, let alone with a loving God who intends goodness for all of us. The beautiful creation of which we are a part includes meanness, suffering, pain, futility, and evil. This leads to questions of who God is and how God operates. These questions are vitally important. And we don't get to figure them out before we start.

Perhaps it would make the most sense to first sort out exactly if God exists and what characteristics God possesses and how God interacts with the cosmos and then we could understand prayer. However, as far as I can tell, it doesn't work that way. Earlier I mentioned that Christian theology begins with the practices of faithful people. Efforts to understand exactly what is implied or affirmed by those practices come second. This is summed up in a very old definition of theology as "faith seeking understanding."[5] One might assume that this means you first have to assent to a bunch of ideas, join a religious community, or sign on to a set of values before you can start seeking understanding. However, if we think of "faith," like prayer, through the lens of relationship, then it becomes clearer. We don't get to know all there is about God before we decide whether or not to have faith. Instead, we learn about God in the process of "faith-ing," of relating to God

---

5. Migliore, *Faith Seeking Understanding*, 2.

Introduction

in the world. McCord Adams's analogies are helpful, again. A child knows little of her parents at birth; a newborn is a bundle of hope and possibility. It is through the daily reality of relating that they come to know one another. One hopes to know a prospective spouse better before committing to marriage, and so there was likely a period of relating before the vows, including a million small decisions to keep relating in order to get to know the other person better. And long after the wedding day, partners continue to grow in understanding one another. McCord Adams states that God is the subject matter of theology (that which theologians are trying to understand) and prayer is part of how we come to know God.[6]

I'm suggesting that we start praying, including talking to God, before we know who God is. This is true for an adult who doesn't belong to a particular tradition and yet lights a candle for a friend going through hardship. It is also true for a small child being raised in a church. The children's minister teaches the kids little songs about God and little prayers to God; it is in the singing and the praying that the children come to have some sense of who God is.

Theologian Karl Rahner says that the word "God" is the term that culture and history give us to ask the really big questions about ourselves and the world. The term "God" helps us ask questions about the meaning of the universe and of our lives within it. History also gives us the word "God" to use when we are talking about aspects of our experience that open up beyond ourselves, which many might call spiritual. We need language to gesture towards parts of our lived reality that defy explicit definition; the word "God" helps.[7] I would add to Rahner's two-fold description of the word "God"; it is also the term that history and culture give us to use when we desire to be in relationship with that which we cannot pinpoint but still feel called to. It is a word that helps us pray.

Electronic Networks

When I first joined Facebook several years ago, I was pleasantly surprised that this social-media tool is so often used for prayer requests. People ask for prayers when loved ones are ill, when preparing for a job interview, when embarking on a new project or adventure. Sometimes people post specifics, "Pray for me at 10:00am tomorrow!" and sometimes not, "Unspoken prayer

---

6. McCord Adams, "Prayer as the "Lifeline of Theology," 271.
7. Rahner, *Foundations of Christian Faith*, 46–51.

request. God knows the need." Often, people make space for various interpretations of what they are asking for, requesting "prayer, mojo, or good vibes." A lot of people are doing something that fits within an expansive understanding of prayer, using a variety of language. Some of these people are "spiritual but not religious." Many have experienced harm in churches or other religious settings. Some never had a religious upbringing; others reject the terms of the religious tradition they inherited. In the midst of all that diversity, uncertainty, and ambiguity, people are reaching out to relate to God, or the Holy, or the Universe—whatever term they prefer—and they are asking others to join them. Remarkably, the communities of prayer that emerge do not require those involved to agree on all the terms—what is meant by "prayer" and precisely who is "God"—in order to be part of the collective communication.[8] Long before all the answers about who God is are worked out, people move towards relationship with God. Drawn by intuition or curiosity or hope or longing—we pray.

The act of prayer reveals a deep hope that God cares for us. Prayer shows the hope and, in some sense, the act of believing that our lives do not play out in a neutral setting or a context apathetic to our existence. In praying, we act as if God is interested in our lives and in us, as if we are already in relationship with God and more is invited. Various religious traditions, including Christianity, affirm this and take it further based on other forms of revelation or knowledge: that God desires goodness, moves toward love, urges compassion, and is justice.

Prayer and Perspective

When we pray, we bring ourselves and our concerns before God—precisely the God who is beyond our comprehension. This shifts the framing of our own existence. It can alter our sense of scale.

Our vision (literal and metaphorical) is usually honed on the midrange—on trees and cars and people and buildings. Given a microscope, we can focus on much smaller realities, on bacteria and cells and such. As I understand it, scientists have not found an absolute end in this direction—more powerful tools help humans see ever smaller parts and particles. Similarly, given a telescope, we can focus on much bigger realities, on stars

---

8. For thoughtful reflection on religious community through electronic networks, see Thompson, *The Virtual Body of Christ*.

Introduction

and planets and galaxies. Our most powerful tools have not found the limit of the cosmos, but instead reveal ever greater horizons.

So as we walk along the street, focusing on trees and cars and other people, we occupy one small strata of an enormous continuum, stretching from microbes to galaxies. It can be awe-inspiring to look up at the stars and recognize ourselves as a tiny element of a vast cosmos. It can, in different ways, help us see our own size more clearly. Stargazing can shift our sense of scale.

In prayer, we put ourselves in intentional relationship with God, whose reality dwarfs the universe and undergirds electrons. God is bigger than the cosmos and smaller than the tiniest particle yet discovered. God is the Creator of the whole continuum. We bring our present conditions, our painful pasts, and our dreams for the future before God eternal, Creator of time itself. Concerned as we are with the minutiae of our own daily lives, we benefit from stepping back to allow our view to include both the small details and the God of all Creation. Prayer involves bringing ourselves and our concerns before the Holy, the mystery of the Universe that holds all things together. This can shift our sense of scale and give us a different perspective on our own realities.

Such a shift does not simply make us insignificant. We already affirm in praying the belief that God cares for us—each and every one. Rather, it emphasizes that we are part of something more expansive than ourselves and that our advocate in all of this, God, is more expansive still. Such a shift of scale does not negate our experiences of pain and suffering. However, these experiences are placed within a larger context that is, we affirm, concerned with our well-being. Prayer assures us that we do not face the difficulties of life on our own. The Holy, God, the Universe—whatever name we choose—desires goodness, moves towards love, and is (at the very least) rooting for us.

Prayer and Formation

In addition to granting us perspective, prayer also forms our habits of mind and emotion. Humans are profoundly malleable. We can be shaped by what happens to us and by what we, ourselves, do. Intentional prayer is a way of shaping ourselves in accordance to the commitments and values that we hold and that are held by our community. Specifically, prayer shapes the

Disciplined Hope

habits of mind and emotion that are sometimes called "affections."[9] For example, gratitude is an affection. It includes both an intellectual assessment that something is a good part of one's life and, in some sense, a gift rather than a necessary outcome. It also includes an emotion of gladness and thanksgiving. If someone makes a point of being grateful for specific things in their life on a daily basis, that person will develop a habit of gratitude, a disposition of thankfulness that will influence how she understands and interacts with the world.[10] The practices of different communities cultivate particular affections. Theologian Don. E. Saliers says, "whatever else it may include, the Christian faith is a pattern of deep emotions" or affections.[11] Christian practices—especially prayer—form habits of mind and emotion that include gratitude, repentance, joy, and love. Other possible affections, such as resentment or disappointment, are discouraged.

Habits of mind and emotion, cultivated in a particular community, are connected with that community's understanding of God. For example, a group that views the Holy as intimately connected with nature might develop affections of reverence for the Earth.

Prayer is a practice that forms affections in those who pray, and those affections cohere with how the one who prays understands God. This coherence is part of a multi-directional dynamism. The one who prays does so in a certain way because of her understanding of God (God is just; I will pray for justice), and praying in such a way shapes her understanding of God (I pray for justice; I see justice as holy). This might seem circular, but it is not a vicious circle, for there are lots of influences and checks that come into play. For religious communities, the tradition itself guides this dynamic with prior affirmations of who God is and isn't. Some of these most basic affirmations are in the form of exemplary prayers. Faithful Jews pray daily, "Hear O Israel, the LORD is our God, the LORD is One." Faithful Christians recite, "Our Father, who art in heaven, hallowed be thy name." Learning how to pray with such examples teaches those who pray about God. These prayers, themselves, are rooted in Scripture, which also teaches Jews and Christians about God. Sacred rituals and writings from other traditions function similarly to convey a vision of the Holy and form members of community in affections that cohere with this vision.

---

9. Saliers, *Soul in Paraphrase*, 9, 27–28, 77.

10. Gratitude has become a topic of much research. Morin, "Scientifically Proven Benefits of Gratitude."

11. Saliers, *Soul in Paraphrase*, 11.

Introduction

Another element in this dynamic is God. When we reach out to relate to God in prayer, God does not leave us hanging. God responds. This means the dynamic of prayer is not a vicious circle, but a back-and-forth of increasing familiarity. Some people hear God audibly; others sense God's presence; some see visions; others simply experience a lessening of burdens or a bit of calm. For most who pray, the received communication varies, and often includes long periods where it seems that God is not present to the conversation at all. Often, prayers for particular outcomes lead to disappointment and feel like rejection or absence. And yet, somehow, for many of us, stubborn persistence in prayer subtly influences our daily lives and our vision of God. We become aware of God as a permanent co-resident of our lives. Drawing again on McCord Adams's analogies, we become aware of God rattling around the house with us, like a spouse or a parent, and we get a sense of God's own habits and peculiarities. They start to rub off on us.

My mother delights in seeing beauty. Her tendency to stop and notice a skyline or to be moved to tears by a sculpture seemed a bit odd to me as a child. As a teenager, I found it ridiculous. Then I started thinking, when I saw a particular tree or painting, "I bet Mom would love this." Now I stop and stare like she does. Furthermore, when I get choked up over a painting at a museum, my tears about the beauty of the painting are also part of my relationship with my mom. Similarly, after years of praying, we are shaped by God's own preferences and quirks. We start to "feel" what God feels and to experience, in some small ways, God's passions.[12] We start to love what God loves. Our hopes and desires imperfectly reflect who God is and what God intends for the cosmos.

Intercessory Prayer

Of course, this can be dangerous to the status quo. Being shaped by prayer can make us unsatisfied with all that contradicts God's loving creativity. McCord Adams says that as prayer attunes us with "divine delight in Truth and beauty, with God's hunger and thirst for joyful life together with all created persons, with God's blessed rage for justice," it also aligns us with "God's apoplectic intolerance of human cruelty and degradation."[13] Intentionally relating to God in prayer heightens empathy—makes us perceptive

---

12. See Harak, *Virtuous Passions* and Brueggemann, *The Prophetic Imagination*.
13. McCord Adams, "Prayer as the 'Lifeline of Theology,'" 279.

to the love and beauty that surrounds us and sensitive to the pain and suffering in our world.

The combination of empathy and intentional relationship with God leads to the particular kind of prayer that the virtual community I'm describing engaged in throughout 2017—intercessory prayer, often including specific requests for aid, blessing, protection, or healing for the person who is the subject of the prayer. At other times, it can be a matter of holding a person "in the Light" or in the presence of God. One can imagine the practice of intercessory prayer as standing in the space between God and a person and bridging the distance.

One of the first questions to arise whenever intercessory prayer is mentioned is "does it work?" What's meant by this question is something like "does what the intercessor asked for actually happen?" Does the person recover from illness, get the job, have a child?

But is this the primary question? Theologian Howard Thurman says that a person who prays does not first calculate whether or not intercessory prayer will be pragmatically effective and then choose how to proceed. A person who prays brings their concerns to God, including concerns for those he loves. In Thurman's words, "[a] man prays for loved ones because he has to, not merely because his prayer may accomplish something."[14]

In my year of political prayer, I let my own intercessory prayers go public. A community of prayer developed in response, as people prayed with me, made prayer requests, and responded. This afforded me a glimpse into the intercessory prayers of others. I've come to believe that intercessory prayer (expansively defined) is extremely common and almost instinctual. When we learn of someone suffering, we want to channel all the goodness of the universe in their direction. We want to comfort them, shield them from harm, and surround them with healing. Our desire for their well-being means that we connect the person, in our thoughts and emotions, with all that we know of goodness and love. And we use whatever language we have at hand—given by religious communities, borrowed from science-fiction, salvaged from a past we barely remember, or invented on the spot—to bring that person to God.

Although we aren't likely motivated by efficacy, we still have the question, "does it work?" Thurman and others agree that, in some sense, it does.[15] However, it is important to be careful about exactly how this is

14. Thurman, *Disciplines of the Spirit*, 101.
15. Thurman, *Disciplines of the Spirit*, 101.

Introduction

affirmed. There are two major missteps to avoid. First, God is not Jeeves. Prayer does not work in the same manner as Amazon Prime, and God is not a house elf. Eternal God, Creator of the Universe, cannot be coerced, manipulated, or forced to do anything. This goes back to the discussion earlier about the ways in which McCord Adams's relational analogies do not fit perfectly because God is not another human person. With a parent or a partner, it might make sense to bargain and persuade and expect reciprocity in many ways. "If you do this, I'll do that," or "if you love me, you'd. . ." But our relationship with God is far more asymmetrical. God's perspective is not ours and God's ways of being in the world are not transparent to our observation. In other words, when we act like God is our wish-granter, we diminish God and set ourselves up for disappointment. The second misstep to avoid is understanding how prayer works in such a way that the logic can be read backwards. For example, the statement that prayer can work miracles, without further nuance, can easily slide into the conclusion that someone who did not receive a miracle didn't pray enough. That is the logic of charlatans. It is victim-blaming masked in religious language. It lies about God (making God our wish-granting servant) and about people (translating suffering into inadequacy). Both of these problems arise from giving our prayers too much power in shaping events.

Theologian John Calvin was adamantly opposed to overestimating our power in relation to God. Emphasizing the glory and sovereignty of God, Calvin said that our prayers do not change God but they can change us.[16] Our pleas will not, so to speak, change God's mind. Another author, Ole Hallesby, makes a similar point but highlights how our prayer does have an important role to play. God always cares for all persons and is always eager to "employ His [sic] powers in the alleviation of our distress."[17] Our prayer does not change God's mind, for God always wills to help us. Praying simply gives God "access to our needs."[18] For Hallesby, God knocks at the door to assist us; prayer grants God admittance.

McCord Adams grants still more room to prayer. God's character and long-term project with humanity is unchanging. God loves us and wills goodness for each and every one of us. Our prayers do not convince God to be on our side; God is already there. At the same time, God aims to be in relationship with us in such a way that we become friends and partners

---

16. Calvin, *Institutes*, II, 852.
17. Hallesby, *Prayer*, 14.
18. Hallesby, *Prayer*, 22.

with God. God aims for friendship across the "size-gap" between humanity and divinity.[19] McCord Adams draws on biblical stories of Moses, Isaiah, Jeremiah, and Job to argue that, "if Bible story leaders are supposed to model being in the world with God, what they model is interaction in which their complaints and protests are heard, in which their preferences help shape the plan, and in which they grow into junior partners in a family business."[20]

In this model, our prayers do not manipulate God, but rather are welcomed by God as collaborative input in how God's unchanging goodness could shape a given situation. I find this persuasive. Whatever God is up to in relation to humanity, human freedom seems to be an important element. Because human freedom makes possible so much suffering—including all the ways we hurt ourselves and one another and the Earth—God must consider it quite valuable to include it in creation. Surely God would then take our freedom seriously in prayer. Put another way, if God respects our freedom enough to allow us to harm one another, wouldn't God respect our freedom enough to accept friendly suggestions on how to help one another? Of course, we remain junior partners and trust God to disregard our short-sighted and wrong-headed ideas.

But what of the apparent failures of prayer? Enslaved Africans and African-Americans prayed for liberation for generations before emancipation. Every day people pray for an end to abuse that does not come, healing that does not occur, and resources that do not appear. There are some times when the prayed-for outcome does occur, but there is no way to know that prayer was the cause. This kind of evidence does not bring clarity.

And yet, many people find prayer profoundly helpful. Many find prayer life-giving and transforming in the midst of terrible circumstances, even when what they pray for does not come to pass. This could fall within the notion that prayer changes the one who prays but does not change God. Prayer provides perspective and shapes habits of mind and emotion in ways that can be powerful. The efficacy of intercessory prayer would require something more than this, because the aim is for prayer to "work" on someone other than the one who is praying. Proving such efficacy would require an impossible level of isolation and control (to eliminate other

---

19. McCord Adams, "Prayer as the 'Lifeline for Theology,'" 274–75.
20. McCord Adams, "Prayer as the 'Lifeline for Theology,'" 278.

Introduction

influences) and a string of assumptions about what would count as a successful outcome.[21]

In my own life, there have been times when I simply could not face or handle situations on my own strength and I have felt buoyed and upheld by the prayers of others. A close friend, Jill, lives with her husband and children in Sandy Hook, Connecticut. Jill is a spiritual person with strong moral and ethical commitments who does not identify with or participate in a faith tradition. In the terrible days after the school shooting on December 14, 2012, when the entire town was reeling with horror, I had no idea how to offer comfort to my friend. I told her I was praying for her. Jill's response surprised me, as she said that so many people were praying for the people of Newtown and the community could feel it. "It's palpable," she said. In ways I can neither demonstrate nor explain, the prayers of friends and strangers provided some small aid in the midst of madness.

Many of us tend to think about how things "work" in simplistic ways. Focused as we are on the mid-range—on people and buildings and cars and trees—we think first of physical causality. A person swings a bat, which either does or does not hit the ball. If the bat does come into physical contact—smack!—the ball changes direction. This is the kind of cause and effect that seems most basic. And yet, we know that there is much more going on in our daily lives than the interaction of nearby physical objects.

With a microscope, we can see millions of bacteria, microbes, cells, and atomic nuclei that are part of the ball field. With a telescope, we can see that the ball field itself is part of a solar system and a galaxy and an expanding universe of galaxies. With different kinds of tools, we could perceive that what appears to be the empty space between the players on the field has a lot going on: oxygen, nitrogen, carbon dioxide, ambient particles, chemicals, gravity, magnetic fields, radiation, radio waves and more. We only see one small segment of light, only hear one small segment of sound waves, and cannot detect much of our environment without assistance. The world is bigger, smaller, and much more complex than we can imagine. Given this, it isn't naïve to think that intercessory prayer works even though we cannot pin down exactly how. Rather, it is arrogance to imagine that what we understand is all that is happening!

I think of intercessory prayer in imagistic terms, quite aware that I don't grasp it fully. God always wills and intends goodness for each and every one of us and for creation as a whole. There is enough freedom around

---

21. Andrade and Rahakrishnan, "Prayer and healing," 247–53.

Disciplined Hope

(human freedom but also evolutionary freedom and perhaps plant and animal and other kinds of freedom that I don't comprehend), and enough history, and enough complexity, that God's will-for-goodness for us can encounter interference. Intercessory prayer attempts to clear the haze and overcome the interference, to make the way a bit clearer for the love of God that is always directed towards our flourishing.

Praying Together

So far, these reflections do not address the aspect of my prayer experiment that I found most surprising and sustaining, namely, the community that prayed together. The relationship analogies from McCord Adams—of partners and parents—tend towards a one-on-one interpretation. Even questions of the efficacy of intercessory prayer can keep the one who prays and the one prayed for as individuals quite separate from one another. In reality, while we are individuals, we are also profoundly interconnected with one another.

We are growing up with millions of siblings, and our relationship with our parents always unfolds in that context. Even the most introverted or isolated among us still leads a life interwoven with others. We become who we are in relationship with parents, caregivers, teachers, neighbors, and friends. We are shaped by the bully in third grade, the heartthrob in tenth, and the one adult who offered good advice. We live our days amidst classmates and coworkers, with fellow-travelers on the train or the highway or the sidewalk. If I tell someone who I am, my narrative will include a whole cast of characters who shape my identity. Even within my own skin, I am communal. I have my father's eyes and my mother's laugh. My sense of humor is a perfect match of my sisters'. I have the genetics of generations, and the DNA of the children I have carried is still in my bloodstream.[22]

All of this interrelation is still on the mid-range—the space of people and cars and trees. If we look at a smaller scale, our intestines are a "biome" of bacteria vital to our health; our bodies incorporate a multitude of microbes that are not incidental passengers, but necessary for our functioning. On a larger scale, our bodies are made of stardust, much of which has origins in galaxies beyond the Milky Way.[23] Socially, culturally, spiritually,

---

22. Doubleff, "Fetal cells may protect mom from disease."
23. Sample, "We are all made of stars."

Introduction

and physically, we are intertwined with the sun and the soil and sustained by the web of creation.

Thurman notes that when someone who prays brings themselves into intentional relationship with God, they will naturally pray for their loved ones. If we allow ourselves to see how interconnected we are, this takes an even stronger tone. I cannot bring myself into intentional relationship with God without bringing the people I love. I cannot pray for myself without praying for my neighbor, because my neighbor's well-being is intimately tied to my own. Omitting to pray about things that influence the community—including politics—would be refusing to bring my whole self to God. It would refuse to hope for God's grace to touch our life together.

Quite concretely, the shared public prayers served several functions. First, they helped form us in hope. Prayer, as a means of formation, instills habits of mind and emotion. The discipline of lifting up a person or group working for the common good broke the temptation to constant fear and anger. It was a daily dose of admiration, honor, celebration, and envisioning a better reality for all of us. Second, it offered perspective. It was easy to believe, in the early days after the 2016 election, that those of us who care for justice and compassion are few and far between. When people said "amen" to the prayers I posted, they let me know they were out there, and they saw other responses, and it encouraged us all. Likewise, acknowledging the people who were resisting helped place the outrageous events of the day in relation to ongoing work for justice that people have been engaged in for decades. It highlighted the geographical breadth and historical depth of justice struggles. Third, it created a space of (virtual) intimacy in which we could speak of things that are often not brought up in casual conversation. Because we prayed together, we were already conversing about big and personal issues, admitting needs and joys and worries. Fourth, praying together created a web of people, from various backgrounds and geographical locations, asking God to help us move the world a bit closer to the creativity, love, justice, and compassion that is, I believe, what God intends. I do not know what piece of advanced technology might be required to pick up on the "good vibes, juju, and mojo" that we sent out to the universe. But just because we can't measure it does not mean it doesn't matter.

There are many stories of hope in these prayers, of small victories, disasters averted, and struggles that continue. For example, on February 24, 2017, this online community of prayer implored God to bless Marty Baron, editor of *The Washington Post*, "with whatever he needs to support and empower investigative journalism." On April 16, 2018, the staff of *The Washington Post* received the Pulitzer Prize for investigative journalism for its "revelations about U.S. Senate candidate Roy Moore" and they "shared the 2018 Pulitzer Prize for national reporting on Russia's interference in the 2016 election."[24] Did a quick prayer on Facebook make the difference? Did our communal discipline of hope for the common good tip the scales? Probably not. But they shaped me, they formed a community, and they invited all that is good in the universe to help us in our present struggles.

---

24. *Washington Post* Staff, "*Washington Post's* 2018 Pulitzer Prizes."

Prayers

January 24, 2017

Every day I will pray for those who resist. Today, I pray blessing and protection for the badass people at the Badlands.[1]

January 25, 2017

I pray this evening for water protectors at Standing Rock, for Boston Mayor Martin J. Walsh, for journalists who tell the truth, and for scientists who protect the data.[2]

---

1. Fears, "For a few hours, Badlands National Park was bad to the bone in defiance of Trump." On January 24, 2017, only four days after Donald Trump was inaugurated as the 45th president of the United States, his administration placed a gag order on the Environmental Protection Agency and shut down their Twitter feed due to information being spread about climate change. One national park refused to be silenced. Badlands National Park in South Dakota immediately began posting a number of tweets and facts surrounding climate change. The tweets were later removed but many commemorated them by creating and utilizing the hashtag #Badasslands.

2. Robbins, "'Sanctuary City' mayors vow to defy Trump's immigration order." On Wednesday, January 25, 2017, President Trump signed an executive order stating that he would halt funding to cities that did not cooperate with his administration's immigration officials. Boston Mayor Martin J. Walsh as well as a number of others made public statements against this executive order and in favor of protecting citizen's rights and the "American dream."

Donald Trump also signed an executive order on this day to allow construction of the Dakota Access pipeline, reversing the December 5th U.S. army corps of engineers permit denial decision (Wong and Levin, "Standing Rock Sioux: 'we can't back down now' on Dakota pipeline fight").

Disciplined Hope

January 26, 2017

Tonight I pray for Louisville Mayor Greg Fischer and every other mayor who is standing up for immigrants. I pray for Dan Rather and for whoever turned Teen Vogue into a political force for good. I pray for every single person calling their representatives. And for artists, of every stripe, who make us more human.[3]

January 27, 2017

I pray strength and inspiration for every writer who is shaping words to resist hate and cultivate compassion, in tweets, FB posts, essays, op-eds, newsletters, blog posts, books, and every other format and genre. I pray for the preachers who are writing sermons that emphasize the consistent biblical mandate to care for refugees. Writing mercies to you all.

January 28, 2017

I pray tonight for all the people who went to airports to protest DT's despicable action, for the taxi drivers who stopped picking up passengers at JFK, for the ACLU, for Judge Ann M. Donnelly, and for all those who participated in local actions to reject discrimination. I pray that God blesses you and adds the strength and power of the Holy Spirit to your efforts.[4]

---

3. Rather, *News and Guts*. In the wake of Donald Trump's tirade surrounding "fake news," Dan Rather began a Facebook group called "News and Guts." Rather stated, "Journalism, real journalism, deep-digging reporting without fear or favor, is as important now, if not more so, than any time I can remember." The page quickly gained over 1.4 million followers.

Beginning in December of 2016, *Teen Vogue* began running op-ed pieces written by staff members with titles such as, "Donald Trump is gaslighting America." Although an unlikely source for political pieces, *Teen Vogue* quickly became a strong, prophetic voice in the resistance to the Trump Administration (Duca, "Donald Trump is gaslighting America").

4. Rosenberg, "Protest grows 'out of nowhere' at Kennedy Airport after Iraqis are detained." Donald Trump signed an executive order on this day in 2017 banning citizens from seven countries from entering the United States. A number of refugees and immigrants were immediately detained at airports across the country. Protests broke out at airports like John F. Kennedy in New York, Washington Dulles, Denver International, Chicago O'Hare, Dallas-Fort Worth, Seattle-Tacoma, Los Angeles International and a number of others.

Judge Ann M. Donnelly, a U.S. District Court Judge, granted a request from the ACLU

Prayers

January 29, 2017

Throughout the day I pray for those in need of protection, healing, justice, and strength. In the evening, I focus on what I am thankful for, and I lift up those people and communities who work for justice and resist hate.

Tonight I am in awe of the continuing protests around the country, and so many friends who are standing with immigrants and refugees. You are amazing. I praise God for your witness.

I pray tonight for Guilford College, my beloved alma mater, which started the #everycampusarefuge program. God bless the people there who are working so hard right now. And I pray for every other school that is rejecting and resisting this Muslim ban. This is important teaching!

I pray also for the Guiding Light Islamic Center in Louisville. The youth of our church visited today, and were greeted with incredible hospitality and kindness. They taught my kids about Islam and fed them delicious food.[5]

January 30, 2017

I pray for courage and protection for all of those who resist. Tonight, that includes the thousands of people who rallied in Louisville. I pray guidance and resilience for the young ones who carried signs saying "Dumbledore's Army." I pray strength for the elders using walkers in the crowd. I pray joy for the Muslim family laughing as they all tried to fit in a selfie. I pray welcome for the people from all over the world who sang the national anthem, claiming a beautiful vision of America as the truth that will yet be. I pray stamina for the civic and religious leaders—Christian, Jewish, Muslim, and more—who call us to our better angels. And for the teenage African-American boy who thanked me for coming out tonight, I pray that he be

---

to stop the deportation of those who were detained. Donnelly stated that the decision was necessary due to the risk of injury that the detained faced if returned to their home countries (Markon, Brown, and Shaver, "Judge halts deportations as refugee ban causes worldwide furor").

5. Diya Abdo, associate professor of English at Guildford College in Greensboro, North Carolina founded the Every Campus A Refuge (ECAR) movement inspired by Pope Francis's call for every parish to host a refugee family. Every Campus a Refuge calls on college campuses around the nation to host one refugee family and assist them in resettlement. To date, Guildford College has hosted 32 refugees total. More information about the program can be found at https://everycampusarefuge.net. Information about the Guiding Light Center is available at http://www.guidinglightcenter.org.

surrounded by so much active work for justice, so much engagement and care by people outside his family, that he someday expects old white ladies to be on the street.[6]

January 31, 2017

This evening I am praying for the Black Lives Matter activists who brought the venerable American tradition of protest into the forefront of our collective imagination. Labor unions and peacemakers and others have kept the tradition alive, but the BLM activists taught a new generation, and reminded some of the rest of us, how to stand up together. When news of this Muslim ban came out, people all over the country made signs and went to the nearest international airport. We knew what to do. We know what this looks like, because we have had such fine exemplars these past few years. Many of those activists have paid—and continue to pay—a heavy price for their work for justice. Tonight I pray help comes at every crossroad, support on every difficult day, concrete assistance in times of need, and a hedge against the evil that always pushes against true courage. I pray they are each surrounded by steadfast companions on this journey, and that joy rises of its own accord.[7]

6. Kenning, "Louisville pro-immigration rally draws 5,000." Louisville, KY, hosted the "Rally for American Values" gathering at the Muhammad Ali Center on Monday January 30, 2017. Over 5,000 individuals gathered for this pro-immigration rally. Mayor Greg Fischer did not declare Louisville to be a "sanctuary city" as many others had this week, but did declare that the Louisville Metro Police Department would not arrest people for immigration violations. Rally speakers included Donald Lassere, president of the Muhammad Ali Center; Rabbi Laura Metzger; Haleh Karimi, executive director, Interfaith Paths of Peace; Shaky Palacios, an immigrant from Mexico; David Yates, Metro Council president, and numerous others.

7. More information about Black Lives Matter can be found at https://blacklivesmatter.com/about/herstory/, including the following:

"In 2013, three radical Black organizers—Alicia Garza, Patrisse Cullors, and Opal Tometi—created a Black-centered political will and movement building project called #BlackLivesMatter. It was in response to the acquittal of Trayvon Martin's murderer, George Zimmerman.

The project is now a member-led global network of more than 40 chapters. Members organize and build local power to intervene in violence inflicted on Black communities by the state and vigilantes.

Black Lives Matter is an ideological and political intervention in a world where Black lives are systematically and intentionally targeted for demise. It is an affirmation of Black folks' humanity, contributions to this society, and resilience in the face of deadly oppression."

Prayers

February 1, 2017

Tonight I give thanks for rigorous historians who offer us facts, perspective, and a sense of how different scenarios have unfolded in the past. Historians teach us about great figures from other centuries, models of courage and fierce intelligence to emulate in our own lives. They also teach us about danger signs and patterns of predictable misuse of power.

I pray stamina for every historian who spends long hours in the library, persistence for the scholars who check the sources carefully, encouragement for young history buffs who are told this isn't a good career path, and patience for those stalwart teachers who strive to hand the wisdom of the ages to students unconvinced of its value. I pray for the non-professional historians—the grandparents, uncles and aunts, and elders of the community who remember the communal story. Here I think especially of Jewish friends whose remembrance of the Shoah compels them to work for justice in Palestine and in America. I think also of families whose grandparents immigrated to the U.S. years ago. The community no longer thinks that this is an immigrant family. But the family remembers the experiences that lead them to flee, the long struggle to get here, the fear and hunger and insecurity. I pray that these historians tell their stories loud and clear. Dear God, please bless me with a history-loving spirit. Bless those who do this noble work. Amen.

February 2, 2017

I ask God to bless those people—over 1,000—who signed the State Department dissent cable. DT makes it a point of pride to harm those whom he perceives to have slighted him in some way. These Foreign Service officers and other employees of the State Department are taking a stand that has significant risks. God, please smooth the paths before them, protect them from meanness, and give them perseverance in this tumultuous time.

I also thank God for the many people who have worked over the years to make the Boy Scouts of America more inclusive. That must have looked like a hopeless battle at many points. Yet people kept pressing, and now transgender boys can join the Boy Scouts. I do not know the names of the people who made this happen, bit by bit, but God does. May they always be greeted with the welcome they worked to extend to others.[8]

---

8. Gettleman, "State Dept. dissent cable on Trump's ban draws, 1,000 signatures."

Disciplined Hope

February 3, 2017

I thank God for humor tonight, and pray God's blessing on every comedian and satirist who is resisting with wit and laughter. Like parents passing out snacks and juice to exhausted children, they give us a bit of sustenance and cajole us back onto the field of play.

When it seems like staying sane and being politically engaged are mutually exclusive choices, humorists demonstrate that this is a false dichotomy. We can be sane, informed, and engaged, but it requires levity.

God, these people offer their light to the rest of us. Grant them deep wellsprings of humor, pleasure, and joy. To every subversive late night host, every funny writer who takes aim at injustice, and every soul who adds to the restorative resistance of hashtag humor about Bowling Green and updates about the current whereabouts of Frederick Douglass, please bring energy and inspiration. Laughter is an antidote to fear. May we fear no evil. Amen.[9]

February 4, 2017

I pray for all the lawyers who are working on behalf of vulnerable populations. The legal system in the U.S. is terribly flawed, but it also marks our aspirations for justice and equity. Many lawyers enter the field to uphold

---

Starting on January 31, 2017, a State Department dissent cable addressing the executive order that banned citizens from seven Muslim-majority countries gained over 1,000 signatures. This dissent cable proclaimed that this ban would not make our nation safer. It became one of the largest protests against the president's policies from American officials seen in recent years.

In 2015, the Boy Scouts of America demolished its ban on openly gay scout leaders. This decision came after decades of activists working through the legal system and boycotting the foundation. Now, two years later, the Boy Scouts of America declared that transgender boys are welcome in their troops (The Editorial Board, "Welcoming Transgender Boy Scouts").

9. Coscarelli, "Kellyanne Conway admits 'Bowing Green Massacre' error." On February 3, Kellyanne Conway, counselor to the president, made the false claim in an MSNBC interview that Bowling Green, KY, was the site of a deadly terrorist attack carried out by Iraqis. The Twitter community, as well as late night comedians, made a number of jokes surrounding the administration's desperate desire to create an environment of fear regarding Muslim-majority countries. Natasha Rothwell (@natasharothwell) wrote, "Saddened and sickened by Frederick Douglass' silence surrounding the Bowling Green Massacre." Jim Osborne (@ozzy4873) declared, "I was a student at BGSU when the Bowling Green Massacre didn't happen. I'll never be able to forget what I didn't see that day."

these values and spend their days pursuing them. God, please grant stamina and energy to these servants of the public good. Help them to be clear-headed, quick-thinking, and creative in their use of legal measures to protect our society's highest goals. Guide those who are judges with your spirit of compassion and your relentless grace.

February 5, 2017

Holy God, I am bewildered. I keep blinking at the screens that show large companies declaring their support for immigrants, refugees, and the value of inclusivity. I am unaccustomed to the idea that multinational brands could take moral leadership. Questions come: Yes, but how do they treat their workers? Yes, but what is their impact on the environment? Yes, but are they just trying to manipulate our emotions for financial gain?

As the questions bounce around, I sense an underlying swell of gratitude. Thank you, God, for the businesswomen and men who are choosing to use their public platforms to affirm the noble values to which our society aspires. Justice. Fairness. The strength of difference in unity. They are, in some small way, reminding us who we say we are, and holding us accountable to that standard. The questions that come to me are valid and important, insofar as they are used to hold these businesses accountable, too. Forgive me, God, when I lose sight of that, and let my critical inquiry become a test of purity. Because rejecting tests of imagined purity—of any kind—is central to the work of justice. I give thanks for help from unexpected places, and I ask God to bless the people of 84 Lumber, Ben and Jerry's, Starbucks, Coca-Cola, Nike, Budweiser, and every other company resisting hate and supporting welcome. Grant them each a double measure of courage and creativity, and may their examples stir the hearts of other business professionals. Let them not grow weary in this work. Amen.[10]

February 7, 2017

I pray God's peace upon John Bercow, the speaker of the House of Commons, who has stated that someone who embraces racism and sexism

---

10. Maheshwari, "Super Bowl commercials feature political undertones and celebrity cameos." Sunday, February 5, 2017, marked the 51st Super Bowl. The Falcons and Patriots played a tight and exciting game that ended in overtime. But the next morning, most news outlets were only talking about the number of politically charged commercials.

should not be invited to address parliament. I don't know anything about this man except this: he is refusing to acquiesce. He is resisting the temptation to pretend things are normal, or to normalize them with pomp and ceremony. God grant him a steadfast spirit, a loud voice, and increasing company.[11]

February 8, 2017

Faithful and steadfast God, please bless every person who persists in talking about the sin of racism that plagues us. In our broken state, we are eager to be deceived, and so we willingly accept nonsense. We imagine that speaking about racism is impolite, and thereby allow racism to flourish.

Thank you, God, that Coretta Scott King persisted in speaking and writing about racism, using her voice and pen to tell the truth and shame the devil.

I ask that you guard and protect Senator Elizabeth Warren. Place around her a hedge against evil. Grant her eloquence; incline the ears of many towards her. Bless her speech with power and her soul with an unyielding dedication to the truth. May she be an example to her peers, and to us, that it may be said of us, "nevertheless, they persisted."[12]

---

11. "Speaker John Bercow defends his comments on Donald Trump." John Bercow was criticized for stating that Donald Trump was not welcome to speak to the British Parliament during his visit to the UK. Bercow stated, "I feel very strongly that our opposition to racism and to sexism, and our support for equality before the law, and an independent judiciary are hugely important considerations in the House of Commons." This comment and others have brought him under fire since his role as speaker of the house requires him to remain politically impartial.

12. Kane and O'Keefe, "Republicants vote to rebuke Elizabeth Warren, saying she impugned Sessions's character." Opposing the nomination of Jeff Sessions as Attorney General, Senator Elizabeth Warren (D-Mass) read a letter from late Coretta Scott King, written in 1986 to oppose Jeff Sessions's nomination to be a federal judge on the grounds of his racist behavior. In a rare decision, Majority Leader Mitch McConnell (R-Ky) interrupted Senator Warren stating that she breached Senate rules by bringing up past remarks about Sessions. Senate Republicans voted to rebuke Warren for reading the letter. McConnell's remarks have since become a "battle cry" of defiance for those who oppose the Trump administration. He said of Warren, "She was warned. She was given an explanation," McConnell said. "Nevertheless, she persisted."

Prayers

February 9, 2017

Holy God, tonight I want to pray for the judges on the United States Court of Appeals for the Ninth Circuit. I ask you—God of justice, mercy, and gratuitous love—to bless these persons, in that mysterious way that you do, providing what is needed even before the lack is felt.

I've said that I will pray every evening for people who are resisting the destructive forces at work in the United States. I am wary that I might insult these judges by including them in these nightly devotions. I do not know them. Perhaps they would prefer not to be portrayed as taking a side in our current struggle. Perhaps they are clear that they are simply following the rule of law—which transcends partisanship—and their ruling today is the logical outcome. Yet such an attitude is, in these bewildering days, revolutionary. Abiding by the rule of law, having three distinct branches of government, attending to the expressed will and concerns of the people, separating the Presidency from business—so that business relations can't influence the president and the president can't influence business deals— these basic tenets of American governance are all under threat, such that anyone who sustains them is a resister. Whether these judges see their actions as resistance or merely competence, I am grateful to and for them. I pray for every person who refuses to be bought or sold. We live in a world in which anything can be commoditized—even our attention—and financial transactions have become a dominant model for human interaction. I pray that our new administration is consistently denied an adequate source of people eager to be bought, eager to sell. Creator God, keep it at the forefront of our minds that we are yours in a much more grounded way. Your claim on us is not ownership, but rather creation and love. We are yours because you made us. We are yours because you love us. Unstoppable resistance can be grounded in this love. Amen[13]

---

13. Liptak, "Court refuses to reinstate travel ban, dealing Trump another legal loss." The Ninth Court of Appeals voted on February 9, 2017, to reject Donald Trump's attempt to reinstate the travel ban, which would prohibit travel into the U.S. from seven majority Muslim countries (Iran, Iraq, Libya, Somalia, Sudan, Syria and Yemen). The court stated that the ban did not improve national security and that there was no evidence that anyone from these countries had committed terrorist activity in the United States.

Disciplined Hope

February 10, 2017

Dear God, I give thanks for all the schools across the country, from Ivy League universities to the Jefferson County Public Schools in Kentucky, that have publicly stated their commitment to immigrant, refugee, and international students.

The current administration of the United States incites fear—fear that demands walls and divisions. Schools are not meant to house fear, but to nurture curiosity. God, you made us curious creatures. We long to know more. At our best, this is not a quest for individual self-aggrandizement, but the communal and collective longing to reach beyond ourselves toward one another and, ultimately, toward you. The educators at these schools recognize that we face global challenges that require global collaboration, challenges that are environmental, medical, scientific, economic, political, ethical, and philosophical. They know that we learn, teach, research, discover, create, and innovate better together. They acknowledge that music blows past borders; art escapes containment; literature calls across continents. Please bless the students, faculty, administration, and staff of each of these schools. Grant them the courage of their convictions, should there be need, to protect the vulnerable in their communities. In particular, I pray tonight for Todd G. May, Chenjerai Kumanyika, and Mike Sears, three professors at Clemson University. Their school has not yet publicly opposed the Muslim and Refugee ban. In order to bring attention to this issue and to encourage the administration to take a principled stand, these teachers began a six-day "Fast Against Silence" on February 6. Matthew 5:6 states, "Blessed are those who hunger and thirst for righteousness, for they will be filled." In order to promote justice and compassion in their school, these teachers go hungry. God, please strengthen, protect, and support these professors. Grant them physical health to endure this discipline. Gather support around them, and let their witness be fruitful in the Clemson community. Amen.[14]

---

14. McKenzie, "Three professors are fasting to protest their university's 'silence' on the travel ban." Three Clemson professors began a six-day fast, starting on February 6, 2017, to protest Donald Trump's travel ban. Todd G. May, a philosophy professor, wrote in an email to the university's president that the university was "normalizing" the ban by failing to speak out publicly against it and by suggesting that some students might be able to finish their education in Canada. "By suggesting alternatives to international students, you have taken a position that is even more consenting than silence," he said. "There are a number of Muslim students on campus who are feeling afraid and intimidated and they're not feeling the support of the university."

Prayers

February 11, 2017

God, please bless all the people who are showing up at town halls, rallies, and protests. It makes such a difference to show up in person. But, of course, you know that.

February 12, 2017

Dear God, please bless the musicians who give us strength to resist, who tell the truth, who cast visions of new realities, and who comfort us in times of suffering. Grant them inspiration. Amen.

February 13, 2017

Dear God, please bless the coders working in Berkeley and some twenty other places around the country to preserve all the intricate scientific data that is now vulnerable to government erasure. They are "tagging and bagging" complex information that could help us prevent still more harm to the earth. They are tracking when data goes missing—as some already has. Guard them, God, as they try to guard your creation from willful stupidity. Give them insight, creativity, brilliance, and good coffee. Let your Spirit sustain them in this work. Amen.[15]

February 14, 2017

Steadfast God, thank you for the elders in the struggle. I am thinking particularly of a woman at church who told me in November that we would have to take to the streets. An activist throughout the sixties, she is deeply

---

The professors also organized a "March Against Silence" later in the month after the fast ended to get more students and faculty involved in the protest of Trump's executive order and to encourage the university president to break the silence on the topic.

15. Molteni, "Diehard coders just rescued NASA's earth science data." Over 200 coders gathered at UC Berkeley's campus on February 13, 2017, to "tag and bag" complex data sets surrounding NASA's Earth Science and Climate Change data. After discovering that certain information had disappeared under the Trump administration, coding and hacking groups began gathering in over twenty different cities to collect and save the data in servers outside the government. In addition to saving and archiving the data, many hackers also built systems to monitor and keep track of what is being removed in order to more fully understand the purge of information.

troubled that she no longer has the physical strength to march. I am also thinking of an eighty-three-year-old man from the same congregation, who has been protesting for the first time in his life this year. He refuses to stand idly by while immigrants and refugees are targeted. God of strength and mercy, I ask you to multiply—exponentially—the power and influence of these two faithful Christians. And while you're at it, please grant the rest of us a portion of her wise determination and a measure of his openness to new ways of living faith. Amen.

February 15, 2017

Dear God, please bless all those whose resistance cannot be publicized. I have known many wonderful administrative assistants and secretaries in my life. They know how things get done. I have been thinking since November that there are women and men behind desks who will misfile things, forget attachments, or otherwise slow down the implementation of new unjust policies. Or perhaps make information known, when not doing so would endanger our democracy. These people probably will not get to feel the life-giving solidarity that is shared at rallies, or to feel the appreciation of others who thank them for their work. Instead, I suspect, their resistance is lonely, and perhaps frightening. I suspect it stems from a sense of duty, patriotism, and an unwillingness to lose one's self through acquiescence.

During WWII, there were several different means of protest. While some people hid Jewish families in the attic, others forged papers, and others publicly denounced the Nazis. One group of resistors, called the White Rose, was made up mostly of about five college students and one philosophy professor. They dared to have conversations on campus, and to produce a series of leaflets urging nonviolent resistance to Hitler. It must have been both tempting and maddening to think that printing some leaflets couldn't really make a difference. Yet they did it anyway. Eventually, the members of the White Rose were caught, to be executed or imprisoned.

We don't look back at the White Rose group today and critique their methods. Well, that might not have been the most efficient, or the most effective, or reach the widest audience, or, or, or. Instead, we look to them with honor and hold them up as examples of ordinary citizens who—in the ways available to them—tried to prevent harm and foster justice.

For those honorable people who use whatever means available to slow the implementation of unjust policies, I give thanks. For those faithful people who use the tools at hand to protect human lives and American democracy—even though no one will ever know—I pray. You know what they are up to, God. Give them guidance and strength. Grant then discernment and protect them from temptations towards power. Keep close to their hearts the principles and peoples who would be swiftly damaged by the new political realities in DC. Protect them, sustain them. Grant them determination and a strong guiding hand. And somehow give them joy. Amen.[16]

February 16, 2017

Dear God, please bless the writing teachers. They know the world does not need another batch of five-page essays on *Moby Dick*. But they believe that learning how to construct a thesis statement, and a paragraph, and to connect subject with verb in a sentence, will help students learn how to think clearly. And the world desperately needs more clear thinkers. Bless the writing teachers with hope and patience, God.

And while you're at it, grant some determination to the geometry teachers who drag reluctant adolescents through the basics of logic. If this is true, and this is true, then you can logically conclude this other truth. Not because we need basic proofs recreated, but because the exercises teach students how to think clearly. The science teachers—please grant them the gift of inspiring curiosity, the tenacity to nourish it, and ample safety glasses. What is your hypothesis? How could we test that theory? Watch what happens. Take notes. Draw conclusions from the evidence. Most of the students will never repeat any specific experiment, but they still learn to think clearly. God, we need clear thinking. And it appears to be thin on the ground, so please grant strength and power, creativity and humor, and a sense of just how vital their work is, to the teachers. Protect those lessons on clear thinking. We need them. Quick. Amen.

February 17, 2017

During the day, I pray a lot of "are you kidding me?!" type prayers, and a lot of "Please God protect" kind of prayers, and a fair number of "may the

---

16. For more information surrounding the White Rose, see: https://www.ushmm.org/wlc/en/article.php?ModuleId=10007188.

odor of skunk fill his nostrils day and night" sort of prayers. At night, I ask God to bless particular people or groups who are resisting the forces of hate and fear around us. It is a discipline that makes me notice those who are working for good, and to hold that which is positive in the light of God's mercy. I post them here because I want to be connected to all of you in this moment. Some of you have found these prayers helpful, and I am glad for that. I try to remember to make them public so they can be easily shared.

This morning, I received a prayer request. A loved one who served in the military was joining other veterans in South Carolina to protest the current administration's policies. One veteran said, "this is horrifying to what WE stand for. It is a disgrace." Another veteran lamented, "It's breaking my heart." It has been a privilege to pray for them all day.

Dear God, please bless the veterans who are protesting. These brave souls have shaped their lives in an effort to serve the common good. When it comes to the aspirational values of the United States—justice and freedom for all—they have skin in the game. And arms. And legs. And lives. The sacrifices they have made on our behalf command respect.

Now, they are fighting for our country in a different way, by demanding that we move towards the values we proclaim and not away from them. From South Carolina to Standing Rock, veterans around the country are calling the government and the people of the United States to become who we say we are.

God, please surround these veterans with your grace and peace. Give them a steady sense of your presence as they, again, work for the common good. Energize them with a sense of community, purpose, and calling. Grant them levity; bless them with joy. May their demonstration of true patriotism instruct and inspire us all. Amen.

February 18, 2017

God of knowledge and wisdom, I pray this night for reporters and journalists. Bless their efforts to know and understand our shared world, to communicate with accuracy and clarity, to provide the transparency upon which the premise of government by, for, and of the people rests. Protect them from harm, as many willingly go into dangerous situations so that the truth might be known. Guard their families, who must worry. And tonight, God, after they have been maligned, give them comfort and sleep.

Prayers

In the morning, please set them on fire with determination to do their work. Give them a collaborative spirit, that their efforts might be multiplied. Guide them to investigate the most fruitful leads, and scatter their paths with useful information. Fill their days with happenstance that points them in the right directions for vital stories. Sharpen their minds to attend to details, and give them focused energy for long hours of research.

The motivation of a little righteous anger would seem appropriate, too, God. But you know best. Amen.

February 19, 2017

God of all creation, please bless the scientists who rallied today in Boston. Give them stamina not only to do the work of science, but to resist this administration's attacks on data, funding, and the very concept of facts. These people didn't sign up to be political activists. But they recognize how high the stakes are at this moment, and that telling the truth is a necessary political act. Grant them encouragement and creativity in the new roles they now occupy.

Scientists exemplify an important virtue. They regularly take in new information and revise their conclusions in accordance with the data. This means they are always open to the possibility that they have been wrong and they are willing to change their views. It is a discipline of humility. God, while you bless these scientists-turned-activists, please grant the rest of us a measure of this virtue. Help us to face the facts around us and to respond accordingly, even when this means changing our understanding. May we be more concerned with truth than status, and may we always seek to know you more. Amen.[17]

---

17. Jan and Cristela, "Hundreds gather in Copley to 'stand up for science.'" Scientists, science advocates, and community members gathered in Copley Square in Boston on Sunday, February 19, 2017, for the Stand Up For Science Rally. In a time when the Trump administration is constantly denying climate change and attempting to erase science and replace facts with "alternative facts," hundreds of people in Boston proved they are not going to accept it. This march is only one of many that took place across the country, all leading up to a larger nationwide march on Earth Day.

Disciplined Hope

February 20, 2017

Holy God, I give thanks for the 16 members of the President's Advisory Commission on Asian Americans and Pacific Islanders who resigned over the injustices of the administration's current policies and rhetoric. I give thanks for Edward Price, who resigned from the CIA after years of service, and for Retired Vice Adm. Robert Harward, who turned down the job of National Security Advisor. I give thanks for all those who are willing to relinquish power and prestige in order to stand for justice.

It is tempting to believe that moral compromise is an acceptable—even necessary—part of attaining influence with which to serve the common good. Honestly, we are all already compromised. We can't pretend our hands are clean. It would be selfish to value preserving some sense of our individual moral goodness over doing everything we can to make systemic changes that would help those most vulnerable.

And yet. This kind of thinking makes it all too easy to ally ourselves with evil, in small, incremental steps.

God, please bless each person who resists the pull of accolades and influence and, instead, is drawn towards equality and compassion. Grant them new opportunities to use their talents, unexpected collaborators, and a sense of peace. Open doors to joyful and surprising places to fulfill their vocations. Amen.[18]

February 21, 2017

Holy God, I ask you to pour blessings upon Linda Sarsour and Tarek El-Messidi, and all the people who responded to their call to action. These two people acted quickly after a Jewish cemetery in St. Louis was desecrated, creating an online fundraiser to repair the damage and communicate support to the Jewish community.

In a time when hate crimes and religious discrimination are on the rise, and when Muslim communities and the religion of Islam have been targets of hateful rhetoric, it would be understandable if American Muslims were focused on their own difficulties. It would be understandable if the climate of fear made it harder to reach out to neighbors. And yet, these two

---

18. Johnson and Entous, "Trump notes new national security list 'in play' after first choice turns down offer." T. G. Lee, "10 Resign from President's Advisory Commission." Price, "I didn't think I'd ever leave the CIA."

particular American Muslims, and many others, are rallying around Jewish communities that have been threatened, harassed, and harmed. Perhaps they know that Islamophobia and anti-Semitism are cut from the same vile cloth. Perhaps they know that dividing the population into separate groups taught to fear one another is a well-worn strategy for social control. But it appears—from the statements to the press and from the warm response of other Muslims—to be simply an outward expression of their faith. Raising money to repair a desecrated Jewish cemetery? That's what being Muslim looks like. These people make me hopeful, God, and increase my own faith. Please protect them and their loved ones; grant them peace and wisdom; let their lights burn bright so that the rest of us might see more clearly. Amen.[19]

February 22, 2017

Steadfast God, I pray for my friends and neighbors in Kentucky who keep showing up outside events where Senate Majority Leader Mitch McConnell is present. Although Senator McConnell was elected to represent the people of Kentucky, he refuses to have town hall meetings. Instead, he only meets with constituents who pay money to attend RSVP events.

God bless the people who show up for democracy even when they have been disinvited.

Grant them relentless and persistent hope. Give them comfortable shoes, friends willing to watch the kids, and coworkers who help arrange schedules. Bless them with energy and laughter, with solidarity and Spirit. Amen.[20]

---

19. Itkowitz, "'Every person deserves to rest in peace': American Muslims raising money to repair vandalized Jewish cemetery." On the night of February 20, 2017, a Jewish cemetery in St. Louis was desecrated. More than 150 tombstones were knocked over or damaged. As police tried to track down the assailants the next morning, two Muslim individuals—Linda Sarsour and Tarek El-Messidi—set up an online fundraising page which exceeded it's $20,000 goal in just a few hours. Ultimately, they raised $162,468, so they were also able to restore another vandalized Jewish cemetery in Colorado on March 24th. Their goal in this project is to spread the message of unity and to recognize that "there is no place for this type of hate, desecration, and violence in America."

20. Tate, "McConnelll goes back to his hometown and finds surly voters." Even though Mitch McConnell now spends a majority of his time in Washington DC, he still calls Kentucky home. When he returned to Louisville on February 22, 2017, he was met by a large group of unhappy constituents. People from Louisville and the surrounding area gathered at the entrance and exit of every space that he was scheduled to speak, protesting and demanding time with the senator. McConnell acknowledged their presence but refused to speak with anyone gathered at the event.

Disciplined Hope

February 23, 2017

Loving God, I pray for every pastor, youth leader, Christian educator, and Sunday school teacher who is preaching and teaching about what faith looks like in our current political situation. Every one who is reflecting on the consistent biblical mandate to care for the refugee. Every one who is reflecting on the grace-filled call to right relationship and the sinfulness of racism. Every one who is reflecting on prophetic calls to justice and mercy. It is always easier to preach and teach a weaker gospel. But it is faithful to tell the truth of who you are and who we are called to be.

Bless these Christian leaders. Give them perseverance in the face of complaints that religion ought not be political, as these complaints ignore both the gospel and the reality that silence is also a political statement. Grant them insight, patience, and good metaphors. Bless them with courage and humility in equal measure.

Triune God, I ask you not just to bless these leaders individually, but also to bless them in relation, giving them strength in community. Give them each, and all together, the power of the Holy Spirit. Amen.

February 24, 2017

God of Revelation, I pray for Marty Baron. I only know about this person through the work produced by the Boston Globe while he was editor (from the Spotlight team reporting on sexual abuse within the Catholic church, for instance) and, more recently, through the excellent journalism of the Washington Post on political issues since he became editor there in 2013. Through his work, I know him to be a leader in journalism in the United States, and someone who is not easily intimidated.

But God, you know Marty Baron completely. So I ask you to bless this man with whatever he needs to support and empower investigative journalism. You know what fuels his work—coffee or anger or good music in the background or prayer or carbohydrates. Whatever it is, PLEASE GIVE HIM SOME. And spread that blessing around. Pour your grace on every editor in every news outlet that cares about factual accuracy. Somewhere today the next great editors of the Boston Globe, the New York Times, and the Washington Post are cutting their teeth on local stories in small towns around the country. Please bless them, too. Amen.[21]

---

21. Hirschfield Davis and Grynbaum, "Trump intensifies his attacks on journalists

Prayers

February 25, 2017

Faithful God, please bless all the community organizers who are working to resist the current administration's harmful policies. Bless those who have been doing this for decades and those who are new to this vocation.

Some of us are used to thinking there are grown-ups in charge and they will do their jobs. Others are used to thinking that the government has never been interested in their well-being. Community organizers take up the task of convincing the first group that their imagined political savior is not coming; and convincing the second group that their own political activism can make a difference.

Creating a real conversation on political issues takes skillful planning, talent, and determination. But it also produces a new kind of community, in which these various groups who wouldn't normally be talking are suddenly in deep conversations while the kids search for snacks. The people who pull that off are community organizers.

God, please bless them with fierce patience. Not patience that waits for change, but patience that fiercely works for change. Please grant these organizers strong faith, creative energy, and a sense of urgency. Amen.

February 26, 2017

Holy God, bless all the artists who tell the truth about the world and help us to imagine new and different worlds together. From the infinite stores of your creativity, inspire those who use their talents in the service of compassion and kindness, justice and mercy. Amen.

February 27, 2017

Creator God, I pray for people who do the math. I pray for the accountants, mathematicians, statisticians, and experts of all kinds who check the

---

and condemns F.B.I. 'leakers.'" Donald Trump increased his attacks on journalists on February 24, 2017, even going as far as banning CNN, The Times, The BBC, The LA Times, The Huffington Post, and others from White House briefings. Trump attacked these journalists on Twitter, stating that they are "fake news that doesn't tell the truth." Marty Baron, current editor of the Washington Post, fired back, calling out Trump's actions as "appalling." "This is an undemocratic path that the administration is traveling," Mr. Baron said. "There is nothing to be gained from the White House restricting the public's access to information."

numbers to determine the likely effects of different political policies and budgetary decisions. And I pray for the non-experts who can add, subtract, multiply, and divide well enough to not be bamboozled.

For every person who has done the math on doctor's bills and insurance payments to get a mistake corrected, or to argue for better coverage. They know healthcare is complicated.

For every person who has double-checked the account balance to make sure the check won't bounce if it goes through today. They pay their bills.

For every person who has saved receipts, pay stubs, or donation records to calculate their tax payments. They pay taxes.

For every person keeping accurate numbers of threats against Jewish and Muslim communities, of hate crimes, and of people of color killed by police and security officers, in order to make the United States safe for everyone. They understand greatness.

Holy God, bless these individuals. Sharpen their minds; guard against errors. And protect us all from things that just don't add up. 2+2=4. Every time. Amen.

March 1, 2017

Mighty God, bless every person who makes the effort to stay informed about politics. It would be easier to look away or to pretend that things are fine. It would be easier both for the residents of the U.S. and for those who seek excessive power. In this context, reading, watching, or listening to legitimate news sources on a regular basis is an act of resistance. Democracy depends upon informed citizens, and faithfulness requires that we acknowledge the suffering of our neighbors. So please bless the newsreaders. Give them accurate sources and stamina to read beyond the headlines. Grant them understanding, insight, and wisdom. Allow them rest and respite when well-being requires limits and breaks. And—in among the stories of meanness and strife—gift them with signs of the Spirit at work in our midst. Amen.

March 2, 2017

Mighty God, I pray for all the congregations around the country who are committed to providing sanctuary for immigrants in danger of deportation.

ICE and the Department of Homeland Security have had guidelines that they would not enter into "sensitive locations"—such as hospitals, schools, and houses of worship—to remove immigrants for deportation. Churches have offered sanctuary to many over the years, providing a haven of safety, time to search for alternatives, and a powerful witness to the love of God.

Since November, the number of churches, mosques, and synagogues committed to offering sanctuary, in some form, has skyrocketed.

God, please guard these communities as they testify to the dignity of all persons. Give them strength, resolve, and peace in their decisions to care for others in this way. Allow their witness to influence their neighborhoods, cities, and states. May their number increase, and their call to compassion grow so loud that policies change and sanctuary is rarely needed. Amen.[22]

March 3, 2017

Eternal God, I am thinking tonight of people who are long-time justice workers who are not at the forefront of the most visible struggles of the day.

Some of them are unable to be as active as they would like because they are tending to pressing matters close to home, like caring for a child, grieving a loss, dealing with illness, or making ends meet.

Others have been steadily living compassion for years, in ways that are rarely in the news. Chaplains, counselors, anti-poverty activists, peacemakers of many kinds.

God, please pour a steady rain of grace upon the people who are in this for the long haul. Sustain them with community; encourage them with surprising kindness; bless them with your Spirit. Amen.

March 4, 2017

Holy God, please bless Stephen Colbert. One of the great strengths of Roman Catholic theology is a global perspective that refutes nationalism and

---

22. Goodstein, "Welcome refugees, churches say in public challenge to Trump." Churches across the United States have formed a grassroots movement to oppose the Trump administration's immigration policies and to offer sanctuary to undocumented immigrants threatened with immediate deportation. As of March 1, 2017, more than 800 churches and synagogues had declared themselves "sanctuaries," offering a safe space to immigrants on the verge of deportation while the legal processes for them to stay are pursued. More information regarding sanctuary congregations can be found at https://www.nwirp.org/wp-content/uploads/2017/03/ACLU-Sanctuary-FAQ-March-2017.pdf.

rejects discrimination against immigrants. It is only logical that when the current administration came after immigrants, a Catholic public theologian like Colbert would come out swinging.

Colbert's fearless attacks on the current administration are not about partisanship or political preferences. They are a continuation of his coherent witness as a faithful Roman Catholic.

Set a hedge against all evil around this man. Guard him from external forces and internal temptations. Continue to grant him inspiration with an open hand. And allow his public witness to inspire us to make our whole lives consistent testimonies of your love for all. Amen.

March 5, 2017

God of Peace, I pray tonight for activist millennials. While there are many forms of internal diversity within the category of a generation, some broad generalizations hold. For millennials in the United States, life has always been complex and ambiguous. Technology, globalization, postmodernism, shifting standards of authority, changing institutional structures—along with many other factors—make simplicity and certainty hard to come by. Millennials are often savvy navigators of a complicated world. And many of this generation demonstrate a kind of moral compass that works in three dimensions—able to account for complexity and still point due North. I am awed by their creativity and courage.

God, please grant them strength and confidence, stamina and humility. Nourish their hope and sustain their work with joy. Amen.

March 6, 2017

God of Grace, bless the schoolteachers who tell the truth about our country's past so that we might have a better future. Give them patience and gladness in their classrooms, support in their communities, and expansive influence in our society. Amen.

March 7, 2017

Merciful God, bless all 100 U.S. senators who signed a letter asking the current administration for "swift action" to find those who are threatening

Jewish communities. This effort is little and it is late, but it is something, and I give thanks.

Grant these senators a firm will for the common good; hinder the temptations to partisanship and political self-preservation. Inspire compassion and strengthen courage. Give them a sense of responsibility and resolve, as well as some common decency and common sense. Amen.[23]

March 8, 2017

God of Wisdom, bless women who work for justice, offer compassion, and love fiercely. Bless those who create, explore, learn, teach, and enact the noblest values of humanity. Let the breath of your wisdom bind them together as co-conspirators for mercy and justice. Holy God, grant them power. Amen.

March 9, 2017

God of Mercy, I give thanks for Congressman Joe Kennedy III, who is resisting the legislation that would strip healthcare from millions of people in the United States. He testified to the biblical commands to care for those in need. He named and rejected the willful manipulation of Scripture into a justification for greed and malice.

Thank you, God, for truth-tellers.

Please continue to inspire Congressman Kennedy. Let his example be a goad to other representatives. May his faith and compassion increase, and may his voice be heeded. Amen.[24]

---

23. Berman, "As more Jewish facilities get threats, all 100 senators ask Trump administration for 'swift action.'" Following attacks on Jewish cemeteries and a number of anonymous bomb threats made against Jewish community centers, day schools, and synagogues across the United States, all 100 senators sent a letter to federal law enforcement agencies urging "swift action" to address the issue.

24. Dwyer, "Rep. Joe Kennedy calls GOP health care repeal bill an 'act of malice.'" The GOP originally proposed a replacement for the Affordable Care Act in March 2017. Congressman Joe Kennedy III called the bill "an act of malice" following House Speaker Paul Ryan's comments that the bill was "an act of mercy." Ultimately, the bill was passed and the Obama-era tax penalty imposed upon those who do not purchase health care was repealed.

Disciplined Hope

March 10, 2017

Merciful God, bless nurses who care for people without judgment. Without asking if someone is wealthy or worthy, without declaring someone undeserving of care due to choice or circumstance, nurses tend the sick and wounded. They offer concrete help and kindness. In this they reflect your own compassion for humanity.

Their actions stand as a rebuke to the notion that healthcare is for some, but not all. May loving nurses receive back the good they have given, tenfold. May there always be someone there to care for them, with kindness beyond expectation. May every pain be eased and every injury healed. Amen.

March 11, 2017

God Who Hears All Prayer, bless those who are praying with their feet this weekend. From water protectors in Washington to protestors in Louisville, people are keeping up the momentum of resistance and showing up to make their voices heard. Pour out your grace upon them, God. Give them perseverance matched with holy impatience. Let your Spirit move among those who march and rally, forming bonds of solidarity that will mark our common life for years to come. Amen.[25]

March 12, 2017

Steadfast God, bless everyone whose cell phone contains the numbers of their elected officials. Encourage their daily calls, buoy their hope, and sustain their resistance. Amen.

---

25. Heim, "Standing Rock Sioux tribe will lead Indian march on Washington." On March 10, 2017, hundreds of activists and members of the Standing Rock Sioux marched in Washington DC and erected a tipi in front of Trump's hotel in protest of the Dakota Access pipeline.

On March 11, 2017, Vice President Mike Pence visited Louisville, KY, to meet with Governor Matt Bevin and local business leaders at Harshaw Trane Energy Management. This meeting surrounded the topic of Trump's repeal and replacement of the Affordable Care Act. Protestors began gathering two hours before Pence was scheduled to speak, demanding that he listen to their healthcare concerns (Kenning, "Hundreds of protesters rally outside Pence speech: 'Save our care'").

Prayers

March 13, 2017

God of Mercy, I pray tonight for states and lawyers challenging the second Muslim ban, for the ACLU nurturing local activism, and for volunteers in programs that reach out to neighbors without shelter when the weather gets bad. In different ways, they all are rejecting the denigration of other human beings and affirming the dignity of all.

Bless them this night. May their rest be peaceful. And when morning comes, may their resistance be powerful. Amen.[26]

March 14, 2017

Faithful God, I pray for Francisca Lino, mother of six, who is facing deportation. I also pray for Representative Luis V. Gutierrez, who staged a sit-in at the Chicago federal building in an attempt to prevent her removal from the U.S.

Please bless them as they strive to keep the Lino family together. Assist them at every turn; grant them unexpected allies; work in miraculous ways to help the Lino family flourish together.

And grant the rest of us a measure of their courage. Amen.[27]

---

26. Grygiel, "Washington, other states seek hearing on latest Trump travel ban." Trump signed a new executive order calling for a revised travel ban on refugees and travelers from several Muslim-majority countries on March 6, 2017. One week later, a number of states (Washington, California, Maryland, Massachusetts, New York, and Oregon) jointly sued in order to stop Trump's executive order from taking effect. Hawaii also separately sued over the new ban stating that these executive orders have had a "chilling effect" on tourism.

27. Mettler, "Francisca Lino, mom of six, is about to be deported. Her congressman protested and was handcuffed." Francisca Lina is a 50-year-old mother of six who lives in Chicago and has been in the United States for nearly twenty years. She was arrested while attempting to apply for her green card. Officers say she lied about previous arrests, but her lawyer states that she was the victim of notary fraud. Representative Luis V. Gutierrez staged a sit-in and was eventually handcuffed and forcefully removed from the Chicago federal building to draw attention to the conduct of ICE officials in Trump's America. Lina was scheduled to be deported at the end of August, but took sanctuary in a church in Chicago. Her lawyer is currently suing on the grounds that the U.S. government violated her Fifth Amendment rights. She is still living in the Adalberto United Methodist Church in Humboldt Park.

Disciplined Hope

March 15, 2017

God of Justice, bless U.S. District Judge Derrick K. Watson, who halted the second attempt at a Muslim ban. He held the current administration to their words—the stated intent to ban Muslims—and resisted the effort to spin this ban as anything else. Grant him strength, protection, and influence.

And may your Spirit empower all those who refuse to entertain foolishness. Amen.[28]

March 16, 2017

Triune God, bless the Dutch voters who resisted hate and fear. Grant us all both individual and collective wisdom in the days ahead. Amen.[29]

March 17, 2017

God of Might and Mercy, please bless Angela Merkel as she fights for refugees. Guide her always towards hospitality and mercy. Guard her from those who are so weak that they fear strong women and suffering children. Grant her influence and power in her efforts to meet the needs of refugees and to call the rest of us towards compassion. Amen.[30]

---

28. Burns, "Two federal judges rule against Trump's latest travel ban." Judge Derrick Kahala Watson is the only native Hawaiian currently serving as a U.S. federal judge. On March 15, 2017, he issued a temporary restraining order blocking the Trump administration's revised travel ban from going into effect nationwide. In this ruling, Watson concluded that the government did not make a conclusive case that the travel ban does not discriminate against Muslims and therefore violates the right to freedom of religion under the U.S. constitution.

29. Rubin, "Trump may have pushed Dutch voters away from populism." On March 16, 2017, Prime Minister Mark Rutte's center-right party won the Netherlands election. Rutte's opponent, the anti-immigration party of Geert Wilder, would have become the largest in parliament. The European Jewish Congress stated, "we hope that this electoral victory will begin a 'domino effect' of mainstream parties pushing back against extremism and populism."

30. Landler, "Merkel meets Trump, the defender versus the disrupter." German chancellor Angela Merkel met with Donald Trump to discuss NATO, trade agreements, refugees, and the fight against Islamic terrorists. The meeting got off to a rocky start when Trump refused to shake her hand. Trump frequently called much of what Merkel talked about "fake news" and told reporters that if they had additional questions, they should ask Fox News instead of Trump.

Prayers

March 18, 2017

Eternal God, bless the volunteers and donors who support Meals on Wheels. Bless the ones who have been supporting this program for years. Bless the ones who just started in response to the proposed budget. Bless the ones who supported this program for two months five years ago and haven't been able to since then. Bless them all.

Grant them nourishment of every sort. Give them company to brighten their days. Let them know that someone cares for them. Afford them dignity. May your Spirit instill in them purpose and peace. Amen.[31]

March 19, 2017

God of Truth, I pray tonight for every institution that has issued a statement resisting the policies and proposals of the current administration. Congregations, denominations, associations, universities—all manner of groups are saying "no" to hate and fear and "yes" to compassion. These statements alone will not change the world, but they are a starting point. They provide a shared vision to which each community can hold itself accountable.

Bless the drafters, the wordsmiths, and the signatories. Give them steady energy to translate words into actions. Amen.

March 20, 2017

Holy God, I pray for Ibtihaj Muhammad, the American Olympic fencer. Her open letter to the current president gave me hope today when hope was rather thin on the ground. As an African-American Muslim woman, she named her religious faith and her belief in the ideals of the United States as reasons she must protest the fear and hatred being spread by this administration.

I watched her fence on television and was amazed by her strength and agility. Reading her letter, I had the same response.

---

31. Carroll, "The cost can be debated, but Meals on Wheels gets results." Donald Trump's first budget proposal to congress on March 10, 2017, identified a number of steep cuts to hundreds of programs in the U.S. Among these programs was the Community Development Block Grants. This is a $3 billion program that gives states and cities more flexibility in how they tackle poverty. Meals on Wheels is one of the many programs that is funded through these grants. Trump's budget, which was deemed the "Starvation Budget," would adversely impact older adults among others.

Please bless this woman. May her faith be strong, her athletic career joyful.

And, God, might I suggest that she feel a call towards political leadership? Amen.[32]

March 21, 2017

Creator God, I pray tonight for the Boston Public Schools. They've recently switched to Peters projection maps, which provide an accurate rendering of land area.

The maps I grew up with pictured North America as larger than Africa. These old-school maps were made for colonial trade routes, so they distort the size of land masses.

Bless the educators who value accuracy and appropriate perspective. May their influence increase.

God, please help us to make accurate maps (conceptual representations) of terrain (facts). Save us from the constant temptation to put ourselves in the middle of things and to misjudge our own importance, either positively or negatively. Show us what is big, what is small, and where our perception is skewed by self-interest. Amen.[33]

March 22, 2017

Loving God, for those who proclaim, in both word and deed, the wideness of your mercy, I give thanks. May even the most faithful find the depth of your goodness cause for joyful surprise. Amen.

March 23, 2017

Loving God, I am thinking tonight of Margaret, a preschool teacher I knew years ago. Margaret has cognitive differences. While the other teachers

---

32. Muhammad, "Ibtihaj Muhammad: I fear President Trump's 'Campaign of Terror' against American ideals."

33. Dwyer, "Boston students get a glimpse of a whole new world, with different maps." The Boston Public School system is believed to be the first public school district in the country to adopt the Peter's Map. The continents and countries in this map are elongated compared to what has been traditionally taught in schools with the Mercator Map. However, the Peters Map is much more accurate and shows the landmasses to scale.

engaged the kids in various creative activities, she counted. Primarily, she counted the kids. Are they all present and accounted for? Then she counted other things. Do we have a snack for everybody? Do we have enough craft supplies? Then Margaret would count the kids again, just to make sure everybody was together, safe, and included.

Her counting was one of the purest forms of care I've ever witnessed. Margaret would not consider herself a political activist, but she taught children an implicit politics of human dignity and the common good.

Wherever she is tonight, God bless Margaret. And bless the world with people who know that everybody counts. Amen.

March 24, 2017

Steadfast God, I give thanks for everyone who communicated to their elected representatives in support of the Affordable Care Act or in opposition to the proposed replacement. Grant us all stamina, watchfulness, and stubborn hope in the days to come. Amen.

March 25, 2017

God of Grace, thank you for those who teach us that play can be a form of resistance, and joy is revolutionary. Shield them, sustain them, and grant them delight. Amen.

March 26, 2017

Holy God, please bless poets. I have been praying for journalists and scientists and those who accurately report facts. Tonight I pray for everyone who has wrestled with words in an attempt to tell more than facts—to reflect and evoke the complexity of reality without diminishment. From the literary giant to the besotted adolescent, bless them all. The journalist, the scientist, and the poet are equally the enemies of lies. Inspire them. Amen.

March 27, 2017

God, Our Refuge, grant grace and protection to every Sanctuary City in the United States. These communities honor the immigrants and refugees in their midst and refuse to acquiesce to heartless deportation practices. I pray tonight especially for New York City and for City Council Speaker Melissa Mark-Viverito, who promised a legal challenge if the current administration attempts to pull federal funding from Sanctuary Cities.

It is not easy to be good neighbors. Pour blessing upon every individual who tries. Send your Spirit to bind together every community that makes the attempt. Amplify our efforts to be neighborly, God, for the forces that separate us can seem stronger than the ones that hold us together. Reinforce our meager hospitality with your divine abundance. Amen.[34]

March 28, 2017

God of Mercy, nourish those who preach the gospel. It is vital—especially now—that preachers encourage congregations to live their faith in concrete ways, to motivate them to action. The easiest way to motivate people is to talk about danger and provoke fear. Yet Christian preachers are called to talk about grace and evoke love.

In the United States, we are accustomed to a motivational logic that says hard work will merit wealth. Gospel logic says that we are given more than we could ever earn; the work to be done is an expression of gratitude, love, and humility; the treasure we enjoy is never our possession. It is a logic of abundance, not scarcity. Gift, not accomplishment. Faith, not fear.

For the people who proclaim such Good News in ways that spark political and social engagement, I pray. Let your Spirit fall upon them as a steady, soaking rain. Nurture them with colleagues and community. Bolster them with joy. Amen.

March 29, 2017

Merciful God, forgive me for not praying publicly for U.S. Representative Maxine Waters before now. Thank you for her unparalleled truth-telling skills. Thank you for her unwillingness to entertain foolishness. When the

---

34. Pazmino, "At sanctuary cities gathering, policymakers vow to become Trump's 'worst nightmare.'" City Council Speaker Melissa Mark-Viverito urged leaders of over a dozen sanctuary cities to be Donald Trump's "worst nightmare" in response to Attorney General Jeff Sessions's threat to cut federal funding for cities for limiting their cooperation with immigration enforcement. Representatives from more than 30 cities around the country were present in the Manhattan meeting.

Prayers

lie that 2+2=5 is repeated so consistently that I start to think I'm crazy, her televised side-eye steadies and assures.

Thank you for her keen insight, deep understanding of governance, commitment to justice, and general badassery. I do not count myself worthy to call her "Auntie," but I am grateful for her leadership in the movement.

Guard her, protect her, set a hedge against all evil around her. May every slight increase her influence; every insult rebound on the insulter to disgrace. Amen.[35]

March 30, 2017

Creator God, bless the businesses, corporations, sports organizations, and artists who refused to do business in North Carolina after House Bill 2 legalized discrimination against people who are LGBTQ. Continue to call them towards justice. In our complicated world, let them recognize their power and their obligations to the common good. Amen.[36]

March 31, 2017

God of Revelation, bless those who ask questions. Bless the curious and the inquisitive.

Asking questions is a characteristic element of humanity. Because we always want to know more, we forever reach beyond ourselves, revealing our holy origins and divine vocations.

When we are satisfied with easy answers and partial truths, when we are eager to be ignorant, we betray our deepest calling.

---

35. Wang, "Maxine Waters swings back at Bill O'Reilly: 'I'm a strong black woman and I cannot be intimidated.'" U.S. Representative Maxine Waters has proven time and again during this administration that she will not back down and she will not tolerate the Trump administration's foolishness. On March 25, 2017, Fox news host Bill O'Reilly compared her hair to a "James Brown wig." O'Reilly later apologized after people responded by calling his comments "sexist" and "openly racist." Waters responded by saying she "cannot be intimidated . . . undermined . . . or thought to be afraid of Bill O'Reilly or anybody."

36. Fausset, "North Carolina strikes a deal to repeal restrictive bathroom law." On March 30, 2017, House Bill 2, the "bathroom bill," which required transgender people to use the bathrooms, changing rooms, and showers that corresponded to their birth certificate instead of gender identity was repealed one year after it was voted in place. This repeal was largely attributed to organizations and sports teams, like the NCAA and NBA, who moved their championship events and All-Star Game out of the state due to the bill.

Spur us to introspection and exploration, God. Help us to ask questions with integrity; sustain us in the tension of inquiry; goad us to know more and more fully. Amen.

April 1, 2017

Holy God, bless those who are willing to change and grow. Grant them the courage of the crocus, the resilience of the daffodil, the extravagance of azaleas, and the tenacious strength of sticky green leaves unfurling. Amen.

April 2, 2017

Loving God, I give thanks for the members of ACT UP, activists who refused to be silent in the face of the AIDS epidemic. In the late 1980s and in the 1990s, they were political and social outliers who misbehaved in public. It was easy to view them as foolish anarchists who were trying to make change in unhelpful ways. In retrospect, their actions—combined with the work of others—saved lives. Bless them with love, kindness, compassion, and friendship. May all their days be filled with holy mischief for love's sake. Amen.[37]

April 3, 2017

God of Righteousness and Peace, I pray for the members of the civil rights division of the Department of Justice who diligently investigated local police departments where abuses where alleged, provided extensive evidence of their conclusions, and worked to enact reforms when needed. May their efforts not be in vain. May their reports be widely read and profoundly influential. May they continue to move our law enforcement towards justice, equity, transparency, accountability, and rationality. When their efforts are derided, hold them up and give them grace. Amen.[38]

---

37. For more information, see http://www.actupny.org.

38 Horwitz, Berman, and Lowery, "Sessions orders Justice Department to review all police reform agreements." Attorney General Jeff Sessions issued a new directive to the Justice Department to review reform agreements made with police forces across the country. Such agreements were developed after evidence of civil rights violations by police officers, in an effort to improve policing and protect public safety. Such DOJ investigations and agreements have led to a number of reforms across local law enforcement departments including major cities like Baltimore and Chicago.

Prayers

April 4, 2017

God of Love, tonight I pray for every person struggling with mental illness. Resistance comes in many forms. Survival and healing are powerful affirmations of human dignity. Bless those who struggle. Surround them with supportive communities; provide them with good medical care; sustain them in the small hours. Let them feel and know your encompassing love. Amen.

April 5, 2017

God of Justice, I pray blessing on the members of the Senate Intelligence Committee. Grant them a spirit of diligence and honesty. May they be conscientious, earnest, and resolute in their appointed tasks. Hold them fast, God, to the work of justice. Amen.[39]

April 6, 2017

Holy God, bless the U.S. Court of Appeals for the 7th Circuit. This week, these judges ruled that the Civil Rights Act of 1964 protects people who are LGBTQ from workplace discrimination. Bless them with joy, laughter, peace, and love. Amen.[40]

April 8, 2017

Holy God, bless those who love. Theologian Karl Rahner points out that loving another human being—really loving them, not just seeing them as a reflection of oneself or a means to an end—is too risky to be wise. People are flawed and finite. Often, they let us down. Always, they die. Either way it hurts. In purely human calculations, love is a bad bet. Rahner says that every time we choose to love another person, it is a leap of faith.

---

39. "Russia 'tried to hijack US election,' says US senator." The Senate Intelligence Committee is charged with investigating the Russian interference in the 2016 election. Investigations began late in March 2017 as Chairman Richard Burr and Vice-Chairman Mark Warner interviewed 20 key witnesses.

40. Briscoe, "Court: Civil Rights Act covers LGBT workplace bias." A U.S. Appeals Court ruled that a federal law banning sex bias in the workplace also prohibits discrimination against employees who identify as LGBTQ.

Disciplined Hope

Explicitly or implicitly, one who loves affirms that there is a larger truth, a wider meaning-making structure, in which the losses attached to love are swamped by love's greater value. Those who love allow transcendent reality to figure in their calculations.

For everyone who takes the risk to love, God grant protection, assurance, comfort, meaning, and a palpable sense of grace. Amen.

April 9, 2017

Creator God, bless those who use the power of twenty-first-century communication technologies for good. We are in the midst of a crash-course on the harms that can be done online. But we also see the positive uses of our electronic connectivity. Protestors who organize events via texts. Justice-seekers who live-stream instances of discrimination to foster accountability. A biblical scholar with mad tweeting skills. And the creative souls who make memes and gifs that tell the truth, alter perspectives, make us laugh, and help us know we are not alone. Bless the tech-savvy resisters, God. Continue to inspire their compact creativity. Amen.

April 10, 2017

Gracious God, thank you for Catholic Workers, whose lived commitment to peace and justice is an ongoing testimony to your intent for the world. They bear witness to the possibility of loving our neighbors as ourselves. Pour out your mercy upon them. Grant them health, wellness, restoration, and wholeness. Encourage them with holy gifts of joy and laughter. Surprise them, God, with abundance at every turn. Make the way smooth before them as they travel faithfully towards the vision of Shalom. Amen.[41]

---

41. The Catholic Worker Movement began during the Great Depression. Dorothy Day and Peter Maurin began a number of Catholic Worker Communities that protested injustice, war, racism, and violence. Today, these "communities remain committed to nonviolence, voluntary poverty, prayer, and hospitality for the homeless, exiled, hungry, and forsaken." For more information, see https://www.catholicworker.org/.

Prayers

April 11, 2017

Holy God, for those who observe Passover, I pray. Remembering—instead of allowing history to be rewritten at the whim of political powers—is resistance. I give thanks for the Jewish witness to liberation from captivity. May your chosen people flourish. Amen.

April 12, 2017

Ever-present God, I am thinking tonight of therapists, chaplains, and counselors. People who accompany others through the valley of the shadow of death, in whatever form it comes. They witness the harms done by injustice, illness, and evil. Their witness is a form of truthfulness; their accompaniment a form of faithfulness. Give them solace and comfort, strength and fortitude. Bless them with experiences of beauty and wonder. Amen.

April 13, 2017

Merciful God, I pray for each person aghast at the suffering in the world. When we are perplexed and near despair, send us your Spirit to guide us towards justice and compassion. Amen.

April 14, 2017

God of Compassion, I pray for those whose lives demonstrate that great strength lies not in the power to harm but in the power to heal, not in coercion but in compassion, not in fear but in faith. Amen.

April 16, 2017

God of Glory, please bless those who celebrate resurrection. Our celebrations affirm that even when all hope is gone and all possibility past, you are still able to bring life out of death and light out of darkness. May we exercise the muscles of our resurrection-hope by living in concrete expectation of your mercy and justice. Amen.

Disciplined Hope

April 17, 2017

Everlasting God, I pray tonight for Kathrine Switzer. In 1967, she was the first woman to officially enter and run the Boston Marathon. Today, she ran it again (for the ninth time), 50 years later.

Bless her with continued health and strength, with joyful companionship, with celebrations to suit her accomplishments, and with ongoing delight in her sport. Bless the rest of us, God, with some portion of her courage in resisting discrimination and of her stamina in continuing to run the race towards equality. Amen.[42]

April 18, 2017

God of Grace, bless those who vote in local elections. Grant them wisdom and perseverance. May their number increase. Amen.

April 19, 2017

God of Justice, I give thanks for those who refuse to normalize sexism and racism. In terms of historical frequency, these discriminatory systems are the norm in the United States and many other places. Yet some brave souls declare that even though sexism and racism are accepted, they are not acceptable.

Bless these courageous people. Grant them healing, for they have surely suffered wounds in their efforts for justice. Grant them comfort, for work that does not have immediate effects still matters. Grant them obstinance, for this is a long road. And please grant them sustaining, enriching, surprising joy. Amen.

---

42. Mather, "First woman to enter Boston Marathon runs it again, 50 years later." Katherine Switzer officially entered the Boston Marathon in 1967 as K. V. Switzer. She made history by becoming the first woman to compete in an all-male race. A few miles into the race an official tried to force her out and her boyfriend eventually had to "body block" the official away from Switzer. Fifty years later, at the age of 70, Switzer finished her ninth Boston Marathon, running the course in 4:44:31.

Prayers

April 20, 2017

Redeeming God, bless the Republican officials who are joining Democrats in demanding the release of the current president's tax returns. Make them resolute in the quest for transparency and truth. Amen.[43]

April 21, 2017

Merciful God, I spent today with people who are devoting their whole lives to justice by working for, with, and through various advocacy organizations. None of their titles sound impressive. None of them are making very much money. None of them have sturdy job security or a fabulous retirement plan. All of them amaze me. Bless those who work daily to influence policies so our common life might be more just, more compassionate, and more joyful. Give them stamina, resources, encouragement, and hope. Surprise them with success. Amen.[44]

April 22, 2017

God of Wonder, bless those who marched for science today. Around the world, in hundreds of cities, people gathered to affirm the importance of scientific inquiry and to protest the diminishment of science through budget cuts and propaganda.

We are surrounded by a world of complexity and beauty. The honest desire to know more about creation is a kind of holy curiosity that gives honor to both God and humanity.

God, please grant today's protestors experiences of awe and wonder at this intricate cosmos, as well as a heavy dose of stubbornness. May such

---

43. Waldman, "Why Tump's tax returns will keep causing Republicans headaches." On April 15, 2017 ("tax day") protestors lined the streets of multiple cities across the U.S. demanding that Donald Trump release his tax returns like every other presidential candidate from the last four decades. Because the Republicans in Congress are trying to pass a new tax reform and tax cut, Trump's personal tax debacle is creating multiple issues across party lines. More than a dozen Republican have joined their voices with Democratic senators stating that Trump should release his tax returns.

44. Every year, Christians from many different denominations and traditions gather to learn, witness, and advocate for social justice in U.S. domestic and international policy during an event called Ecumenical Advocacy Days. From April 21–24, advocates gathered in Washington, DC to work against racism, materialism, and militarism. For more information, see https://advocacydays.org/2017-confronting-chaos/.

Disciplined Hope

protests help us find one another—to meet the people in our communities who have shared values and concerns—that we might develop strong and lasting relationships of solidarity. Amen.[45]

April 23, 2017

God of Hope, bless Amal Nassar, a Palestinian farmer. She and her family grow fruit and olives on their ancestral land near Bethlehem. As they have for over a hundred years.

When the occupying military forces come in the middle of the night and bulldoze olive trees, the Nassar family plants new ones.

Their farm, the Tent of Nations, is also an educational center that teaches international visitors and volunteers about nonviolence, love of the land, and peacemaking. Their motto is, "We refuse to be enemies."

I do not understand faith this strong or deep, God. It is beyond me.

Please bless Amal and the Nassar family. Bless their land and their trees. Bless the Tent of Nations and all who visit and learn there. Bless the Palestinian people. And God, please bless the rest of us with enough sense, vision, and compassion to reject apartheid in any form and to work actively for just peace. Amen.[46]

April 24, 2017

Merciful God, bless the Christians from all over the country who lobbied congress today under the auspices of Ecumenical Advocacy Days. Help us continue to work together for the common good. May our efforts yield good fruit through your power. Amen.[47]

---

45. St. Fleur, "Scientists and activists look beyond the March for Science." Scientists and science advocates filled the streets of more than 500 cities worldwide in support of research and scientific advocacy, which has diminished under the Trump administration. On Saturday, April 22, 2017 (Earth Day), people gathered to protest the administration's orders to stop federal agencies from informing the public regarding scientific topics like climate change and to demand "Science, not Silence!"

46. Learn more at http://www.tentofnations.org.

47. Christians nationwide gathered April 21–24 for Ecumenical Advocacy Days to focus on the theme "Confronting Chaos, Forging Community." Throughout the weekend, the group wrestled with the intersectionality of racism, materialism, and militarism. The last day, Monday, April 24th, culminated with Lobby Day, where participants met on Capitol Hill to speak with members of the Senate and Congress. A group of dozens of

Prayers

April 26, 2017

God of Mercy, bless William H. Orrick, the federal judge who ordered a temporary injunction against the current administration's efforts to withhold federal funding from sanctuary cities.

Bless those who protect the most vulnerable among us.
Bless those who reject doublespeak.
Bless those who have integrity in their professions.
Amen.[48]

April 27, 2017

Loving God, I pray for the members of Congress who support the Therapeutic Fraud Prevention Act of 2017, which would ban the harmful practices known as "conversion therapy," "reparative therapy," or "ex-gay therapy."

May these legislators be blessed with communities where children and teens are not abused by so-called therapists who offer nothing but pain and shame. May their districts experience shocking decreases in suicide attempts and bullying. May their own families flourish, and may they develop a strong taste for justice. Amen.[49]

Christian clergy and lay leaders and advocates also participated in prayerful witness and civil disobedience in a Senate office building, rejecting the budget proposal of President Trump that calls for reduction in human-needs spending at home and abroad to pay for sharp and unnecessary increases in Pentagon spending. For more information, see https://advocacydays.org/2017-confronting-chaos.

48 Yee, "Judge blocks Trump effort to withhold money from sanctuary cities." William H. Orrick of the United States District Court in San Francisco temporarily blocked Donald Trump's efforts to suppress federal funding from areas that limit their cooperation with immigration enforcement. Judge Orrick stated that only Congress could place the conditions on spending and therefore that the president had overstepped his powers in doing so.

49. Wang, "Supreme Court upholds California's ban on gay 'conversion therapy.'" "Conversion Therapy" is a practice that has been deemed "harmful and misleading" by mental-health professionals and LGBTQ rights groups. This therapeutic practice claims to be able to change a person's sexual orientation or gender identity. About 70 members of congress, all Democrats, put their support behind the Therapeutic Fraud Prevention Act of 2017, which was introduced on April 27th. This bill would allow the Federal Trade Commission to classify conversion therapy as fraudulent because it is treating someone for a medical condition that does not exist.

Disciplined Hope

April 28, 2017

Loving God, I lift up Bishop Karen Oliveto, a faithful servant of the church, and those within the United Methodist Church who elected and consecrated her to that position. I lift up all LGBTQ members of the UMC, especially those ordained to ministry.

Make your gracious presence keenly felt as they face discrimination and insult. Surround them with your blessing. Let your fierce love for each of them be known. Amen.[50]

April 29, 2017

Creator God, bless those who participated in the People's Climate March, protesting the current administration's denial of climate change and destructive environmental policies.

Grant these marchers stamina for the struggle, insight into effective strategies, broad influence, and deep hope. Amen.[51]

April 30, 2017

God of Wisdom, bless all those who are intentionally learning about how racism functions in our society so they can work for justice. I pray for the thousands gathered in Kansas City at the White Privilege Conference, for the twelve people in a book group in Charlotte, for the seminary students who sign up for classes that scare them, and for the individuals who listen when injustice is named. Grant us both humility and hope. Amen.[52]

50. Bloom, "Consecration of gay bishop against church law." Rev. Karen Oliveto was consecrated as a bishop in the United Methodist Church on July 16, 2016. Just nine months later, on April 28, 2017, the judicial council ruled that the "consecration of a gay bishop violates church law, but the bishop remains in good standing until an administrative process is complete." Oliveto, who is married to Robin Ridenour, was consecrated to the position despite being openly gay. A different jurisdiction, the South Central Jurisdiction, raised the question of the legality of this election, which ultimately led to the UMC's ruling of violation.

51. Fandos, "Climate March draws thousands of protesters alarmed by Trump's environmental agenda." Thousands of protestors took to the streets of Washington DC near the Capitol on the president's 100th day in office in order to object to Donald Trump's environmental policies that have prioritized immediate economic growth over environmental concerns.

52. Robertson, "Got Privilege? Kansas City preparing to host the national White

Prayers

May 1, 2017

Triune God, I give thanks for labor organizers and union members. Bless those who have gone before and those who continue the efforts today. Bless those who stand together in solidarity for justice.

Grant them stamina in the face of decades-long assaults on organized labor. Give them strength to work together and to resist the "every man for himself" mentality that weakens us all. Pour your Spirit out among them, God, and give them grace. Amen.

May 2, 2017

God of Wisdom, bless librarians. They safeguard the best of human achievement and ideals. Please give them ample funding, quiet patrons, and good bourbon. Amen.

May 3, 2017

Mighty God, bless the faith leaders in Texas who are resisting so-called "religious freedom" bills being put forth in the state. They know that such bills are not about religious freedom at all, but rather promise license to discriminate, white-washed in the language of religion.

For those who refuse to use you as a justification for hatred, I give thanks. Give them strength and stubbornness. Multiply their number and increase their power. Amen.[53]

Privilege Conference." April 27–30, 2017, the 18th annual White Privilege Conference was held in Kansas City, MO. This is a conference "that examines challenging concepts of privilege and oppression" to build strategies "toward a more equitable world." In 2016, the conference drew more than 2,500 people, from students to teachers and administrators to social activists, clergy, and business people.

53. Ura, "Texas faith leaders come out against bills targeted at LGBT Texans." Conservative lawmakers in Texas unveiled a number of "religious freedom" bills on Wednesday, May 3, 2017, including one known as FADA—the First Amendment Defense Act. These bills, which are being promoted under the guise of religion, allow individuals and businesses to refuse service to same-sex couples based on their belief that marriage should be between one man and one woman. Many faith leaders across the state made it known that they did not support this slate of anti-LGBTQ bills.

Disciplined Hope

May 4, 2017

God of Healing, I pray for voters. Bless them with long memories. Amen.

May 5, 2017

Gracious God, please bless everyone who manages to be kind. I especially lift up Kathy, a stranger who was nice for no reason. May those who offer kindness be surrounded by it. Amen.

May 7, 2017

God of Hope, bless the voters of France. May they continue to reject hatred and fear as a form of governance. Grant them constructive vision for a just future, collective will to seek it, and creative opportunities to move towards it. Amen.[54]

May 8, 2017

Holy God, bless Sally Yates for every bit of truth she told today. Actually, bless everyone who told—or sought—the truth today. Grant us all a desire for honesty, knowledge, and wisdom. Amen.[55]

May 9, 2017

Sweet Baby Jesus, if there is anyone in the government of the United States (including all three branches and right down to Leslie Knope) who has an

---

54. Aisch, Bloch, LaI, and Morenne, "How France voted." The 2017 French presidential election caught the world's attention in new ways due to the stark differences between the candidates. Marine Le Pen, a far-right candidate, promised to pull France out of NATO's military command, the euro zone, and the European Union. Emmanuel Macron, a centrist with a moderate stance on economics and social issues, won the election.

55. Apuzzo and Huetteman, "Sally Yates tells senators she warned Trump about Michael Flynn." Former acting Attorney General Sally Yates, who was fired by Trump, testified in front of a Senate subcommittee about Michael Flynn's ties to Russia. This testimony pulled the story of the Trump campaign's alleged ties to Russia back into the headlines. Yates stated that Flynn could be "blackmailed by the Russians because he misled the vice president about his problematic conduct."

Prayers

ounce of integrity, please bless them with motivation and focus to fully investigate this Russia mess. We are way past enough already. Amen.

May 10, 2017

Holy God, bless Senator John McCain, who appears to be the moral backbone of the Republican party. Grant him strength of purpose as he calls for a select committee to investigate ties between Russia and the current administration. Protect him from pressure to acquiesce with deception. Provide him wise counselors and steadfast friends. Preserve his dedication to democracy, transparency, and rule of law. Amen.[56]

May 11, 2017

God of Righteousness and Peace, bless the 2017 graduates of Bethune-Cookman University, a historically black institution. These graduates refused to normalize the appointment of an unqualified person to the post of Education Secretary by sitting quietly through Betsy DeVos's commencement address. Instead, they turned their backs to her. Not polite, but neither was overturning tables in the temple. May the Spirit of justice continue to move among these graduates.

Please also bless the 215 black professors who signed a moving letter of approbation to these graduates. Amen.[57]

---

56. Rogin, "John McCain on Comey firing: 'There will be more shoes to drop.'" Senator McCain warned a group of foreign diplomats that the controversy surrounding Donald Trump firing FBI Director James Comey would continue. He also compared the situation to the "Saturday Night Massacre" where President Nixon fired the prosecutor investigating Watergate. In a statement made on May 9, 2017, Senator McCain called for a special congressional committee to investigate Russia's interference in the 2016 election, stating that "Comey's termination only confirms the need and urgency of such a committee."

57. Green, "Bethune-Cookman graduates greet Betsey De Vos with turned backs." Bethune-Cookman University graduates turned their backs and walked out during Education Secretary Betsy DeVos's commencement speech. In the weeks leading up to this speech, students and alumni protested her scheduled appearance. In February, DeVos was quoted stating, "Historically black colleges and universities are real pioneers when it comes to school choice."

Disciplined Hope

May 12, 2017

God of Wisdom and Delight, bless the person or persons behind Merriam-Webster's twitter account. When the current occupant of the White House mangles language—especially when he does so in a misleading or deceptive fashion—the good people at Merriam-Webster tweet accurate definitions and etymologies.

The dictionary has taken up its place in the resistance. Amen.[58]

May 13, 2017

Merciful God, bless John Oliver. He gambled his career on the belief that a significant number of people in the U.S. would tune in for a lecture once a week. A witty lecture, yes, but fundamentally didactic. He makes us laugh and offers us the knowledge necessary to participate in shaping our shared world. Please grant this quirky person a large classroom of eager learners. Inspire and guide him. Continue to give him clear vision and fierce hope. And while you're at it, please give the rest of us enough bandwidth to protect net neutrality. Amen.

May 14, 2017

God of Creativity and Hope, bless the graduates. Work with and through them to make the world a more just, compassionate, and joyful place. Amen.

May 15, 2017

God of Wisdom, bless Barbara Rank, a retired special education teacher who wrote a brief letter to her local paper in response to a congressman's claim that it is crazy to mandate that insurance cover pregnancy. Ms Rank's concise and elegant letter included these words: "It's called democracy, a civil society, the greater good." Please surround Ms. Rank with thoughtful people who appreciate her literary skills. Encompass her with a community

---

58. Raphelson, "The Merriam-Webster Dictionary has been trolling Trump on Twitter for months."

Prayers

that strives for the greater good. May her sturdy wisdom be contagious. Amen.[59]

May 16, 2017

Holy God, keep it coming with the journalists. Give them dogged perseverance, reliable sources, desire for truth, and a keen sense of duty. Amen.

May 17, 2017

God of Healing, I pray for this brave woman, Molly Young. In the midst of her own struggle with breast cancer, she is resisting the repeal of the Affordable Care Act, aka Obamacare.

May her doctors, nurses, and other medical caregivers be ridiculously brilliant and skillful. May her body respond wonderfully to the treatment and medication. May she be surrounded by supportive family and friends. May she look back with pride—decades from now—knowing that she helped prevent devastating cuts to affordable healthcare. Amen.

May 18, 2017

Creator God, I pray for those who resist our current political fiasco by running for office. Lift those who have a heart for public service. Encourage those who value democracy. Sustain those who invest their time and energy into the common good. Amen.

May 21, 2017

Steadfast God, bless the Notre Dame graduates who protested when Mike Pence spoke at their commencement. It was a peaceful demonstration of their support for the LGBTQ community as well as their dissatisfaction with the policies and rhetoric of the current administration.

May these graduates continue to engage the political realities that cause harm to neighbors, friends, and family members. Grant them compassion for all who are vulnerable. Give them persistent strength to work

---

59. Rank, "Letter: Why should I pay indeed?"

Disciplined Hope

for justice. Let their example spur the rest of us to make our voices heard. Amen.[60]

June 5, 2017

Creator God, I pray for every mayor, university president, governor, and business person who has pledged to meet the goals laid out in the Paris Climate Accord. May they be unyielding in their commitment to our common home. Grant them ingenuity and a vibrant sense of shared purpose. Amen.[61]

June 6, 2017

Creator God, bless David Rank, a Foreign Service diplomat who has been the acting U.S. ambassador to China. Rank resigned this week because he could not, in good conscience, take part in implementing the current administration's withdrawal from the Paris Climate Accord. It is reported that Rank's identity as a parent and a Christian influenced his decision. May he live to see a true and active global commitment towards caring for the Earth. Amen.[62]

June 7, 2017

God of Grace, I pray tonight for the Republican legislators in Kansas who are recognizing that the extreme tax-cut experiment of Gov. Brownback has failed. It takes strength to change course. Bless those who are willing

---

60. Stack, "Notre Dame students walk out of Mike Pence commencement address." Over 100 students quietly stood up and walked out as vice president Mike Pence began his commencement speech at the 172nd commencement ceremony at Notre Dame. Many students have been personally impacted by the policies put in place during Pence's time as Indiana governor, especially those targeting people who identify as LGBTQ and families who have undocumented members.

61. Popoich and Schlossberg, "How cities and states reacted to Trump's decision to exit the Paris climate deal." Donald Trump announced on June 5, 2017, that he was pulling the U.S. out of the Paris Climate Accord. Trump claimed that the pact hurts American workers and puts "draconian" financial burdens on the U.S. It will take almost four years to get out of the accord, until November 2020.

62. Rank, "Why I resigned from the Foreign Service after 27 years."

to learn. May we all be open to reconsidering our positions in light of data. Amen.[63]

June 8, 2017

God of Mercy, bless Court Appointed Special Advocate (CASA) volunteers as they look out for the interests of abused or neglected children in legal proceedings. Heroes walk among us. Amen.[64]

June 9, 2017

God of Hope, I pray for the young people of Britain who voted in this election. Some estimates put young voter turnout at 72 percent.

Bless them with compassion, thoughtfulness, curiosity, honesty, and ongoing commitment to civic engagement. May their examples inspire others, even an ocean away. Amen.[65]

June 10, 2017

God of Truth, bless Senator Kirsten Gillibrand, who recently said of Congress, "Fundamentally, if we are not helping people, we should go the fuck home." That sums things up nicely. Amen.[66]

June 11, 2017

Gracious God, bless Jimmy Carter, who made the news this weekend for his kindness. In his consistent efforts on behalf of those who are poor and those who are sick, President Carter has been an exemplar of Christian values. His advocacy on behalf of the environment was groundbreaking. On

---

63. Bosman, Smith, and Davey, "Brownback tax cuts set off a revolt by Kansas Republicans." Kansas legislators voted on June 6, 2017, to roll back Governor Sam Brownback's 2012 tax cuts, which had been an experiment in conservative economics that led to massive budget shortfalls.

64. To learn more about the CASA program, go to http://www.casaforchildren.org/.

65. Yeginsu, "What turned the British election? Maybe the youth vote." The young voter turnout in the 2017 UK general election was greater than at any other point in the last 25 years.

66. Phillips, "This Democratic senator's thoughts on Trump? We can't write it here."

matters of race and gender, he became a steadfast ally, standing for justice even when the personal cost was high. Throughout, President Carter has embodied a deep Christian faith that has no need to compete with other religious traditions.

It was a blessing to see his photo in the newspaper and be reminded of his powerful witness for compassion and peace.

Please surround Jimmy and Rosalynn Carter with love, hope, joy, and peace. Amen.[67]

June 12, 2017

Holy God, I pray for the Attorney General of Maryland, Brian Frosh, and the Attorney General of DC, Karl Racine. They have filed a lawsuit against the current occupant of the White House for violating the emoluments clause of the Constitution, which states that a president cannot receive funds from foreign governments or officials, as this would invite corruption and influence peddling. Aid them in their efforts to uphold the best of our democracy. Amen.[68]

June 13, 2017

Holy God, I pray for the bean-counters, the note-takers, the record-keepers, and the fact-checkers. For those who care about accuracy and detail. May they have voice and influence in the days ahead. Amen.

June 14, 2017

God of Mercy, I pray tonight for the members of Sandy Hook Promise, an organization formed by parents and spouses who lost loved ones in the

---

67. Chavez, "Jimmy Carter greets every passenger on flight from Atlanta to DC." Former President Jimmy Carter made headlines on June 11, 2017, for stopping to shake every passenger's hand aboard a Delta Airlines flight. Numerous passengers Tweeted about and took videos of President Carter's kindness, noting that this was not the first time that he has done this; apparently this is an airplane ritual for Carter, along with flying coach.

68. Davis, "D.C. and Maryland sue President Trump, alleging breach of constitutional oath." The attorneys general of Maryland and DC filed a lawsuit on Monday, June 5, 2017, claiming that government payments to Donald Trump's businesses violate the U.S. Constitution. Foreign and domestic government payments to Trump's businesses became the target of a similar lawsuit brought in January by ethics nonprofit groups.

shooting in Newtown, Connecticut, in 2012. They aim to protect children from gun violence through programs including education and advocacy for sensible policies.

In the midst of mourning and lament, they moved toward peace, compassion, and care for others. May their efforts inspire us and bear fruit. Amen.[69]

June 15, 2017

God of Knowledge, bless the senators—both Democrat and Republican—who are resisting Mitch McConnell's attempt to write and pass a healthcare bill in secret. May their efforts draw attention to this end run around democracy. Amen.[70]

June 17, 2017

Triune God, I give thanks for Nikos Giannopoulos, Rhode Island Teacher of the Year, who made sure his photograph in the Oval Office reflected his queer identity. In Beacon Charter High School for the Arts, Giannopoulos encourages and advocates for LGBTQ students. His approach to a single photo op brought the rest of us into his classroom, as he demonstrated how to act in courage, joy, and resistance all at once. Shield him from hatred; surround him with love. May his work improve the lives of all who learn from him. Amen.[71]

---

69. To learn more about Sandy Hook Promise, go to http://www.sandyhookpromise.org.

70. Slavitt, "The Senate's three tools on health care: Sabotage, speed, and secrecy." Republicans attempted to take an unprecedented step by passing a bill to eliminate health insurance from millions of Americans without a single hearing. Senate Majority Leader Mitch McConnell kept his bill secret and attempted to rush it into law in an effort to draw minimal public scrutiny. His defended the secrecy with claims that this debate has been going on for the last seven years and that there have already been "gazillions of hearings on this subject."

71. Selk, "A teacher's decision to be 'visibly queer' in his photo with President Trump." Nikos Giannopoulos, or "Mr. G" as his students call him, leads the gay-straight alliance at Beacon Charter High School for the Arts in Rhode Island. On June 17, 2017, he was photographed with Donald and Melania Trump in the Oval Office. He decided to use the opportunity to represent the LGBTQ community. "I wore a rainbow pin to represent my gratitude for the LGBTQ community that has taught me to be proud, bold and empowered by my identity—even when circumstances make that difficult." Giannopoulos said

Disciplined Hope

June 17, 2017

God, our souls ache. Help us.

Black Lives Matter is a theological claim. We know black lives don't matter to many people and in many systems. But we attest that those people and systems are wrong, because Black Lives Matter ultimately. A Christian way of saying that is Black Lives Matter to God, to you, the measure of all.

When our souls ache with sorrow and outrage, it is faith that makes them so. In faith, we know we are called to be better than this. We know that this unrelenting pattern of black men, women, and children being killed by security and law-enforcement officers is contrary to your will.

Ease our sorrow and anger by helping us to change the world. Amen.

June 18, 2017

Everlasting God, bless the people of NBC Connecticut who decided not to air Megyn Kelly's interview with a hate-monger. In the five years since the school shooting in Newtown, bereaved parents have been tormented by gullible and vicious strangers who believe the shooting never happened. NBC Connecticut will not grant a platform to a person who spouts such harmful lies. May the practice of valuing truth over profit be contagious. Amen.[72]

June 19, 2017

God of Grace, bless the members of the Presidential Advisory Council on HIV/AIDS who resigned in protest against the current administration's complete lack of care for people suffering from this disease: Scott Schoettes, Lucy Bradley-Springer, Gina Brown, Ulysses W. Burley III, Grissel

---

he wore "a blue jacket with a bold print and carried a black lace fan to celebrate the joy and freedom of gender nonconformity."

72. Segarra, "Connecticut NBC affiliate will not air Megyn Kelly's Alex Jones interview." On Sunday night, June 18, 2017, Megyn Kelly's special interview with Infowars founder and conspiracy theorist Alex Jones aired nationwide. Jones said he believed that the Sandy Hook Elementary School shooting in Newtown, Connecticut, was a government hoax that used child actors. Connecticut's NBC affiliate WVIT decided not to air the interview stating, "Over the last few days, we have listened intently to Sandy Hook parents and considered the deep emotions from the wounds of that day that have yet to heal."

Granados, and Michelle Ogle. Grant them opportunities to continue their advocacy and success in their efforts to curtail HIV/AIDS. Amen.[73]

June 20, 2017

God of New Life, bless Randy Bryce, an Army veteran, iron-worker, and union leader who has announced he will run against Paul Ryan in 2018.

I don't know Bryce, but I do know what Ryan has done and is currently doing in office. I ask your blessing on everyone who runs, campaigns, volunteers, and votes in order to change things for the better. May 2018 be a year of powerful compassion and mighty solidarity. Amen.[74]

June 21, 2017

God of Abundant Life, I give thanks for Rida Hamida and Ben Vazquez, organizers of a campaign in California called Taco Trucks at Every Mosque. During the month of Ramadan, Latinos/as/x invite Muslims to a meal of delicious halal tacos at sunset, when those observing the holy month break fast. It is an opportunity for these two communities—which already overlap—to develop friendships and solidarity in a political moment when they are both being targeted.

Please bless Hamida and Vazquez with strength and joy. May their creativity, hope, compassion, and hard work bear fruit. Amen.[75]

---

73. Ogle, "Six members of the Presidential Council on HIV/AIDS resign." When Dr. Michelle Ogle was asked why she left the Presidential Advisory Council on HIV/AIDS, she was quoted saying Donald Trump, "simply does not care about the issue." This quote comes after Ogle reported that Trump refused to meet with the advocates and stakeholders, as well as interpreting Trump's budget proposal and the American Health Care Act bill that he had put forward that did not take HIV/AIDS into consideration.

74. Mettler, "This union ironworker wants Paul Ryan's job. He's got a great ad but a losing record." Randy Bryce unveiled his new campaign advertisement on June 20, 2017, issuing a challenge to Speaker Paul Ryan. "Let's trade places, Paul Ryan," Bryce says, "You can come work the iron, and I'll go to DC." The ad also features Bryce's mother, who suffers from multiple sclerosis, and a scathing review of the Republicans' health care plans.

75. Bharath, "Santa Ana mosque members break Ramadan fast with tacos."

Disciplined Hope

June 22, 2017

God of Strength, I pray for those who demonstrated outside Mitch McConnell's office to protest the Republican healthcare bill in the Senate. Many of those present use wheelchairs or breathing machines. The legislation would drastically reduce Medicaid, which provides care for many people with disabilities, while giving a large tax break to the very wealthy. Police arrested 43 people, separating several from their wheelchairs and leaving blood on the floor.

Pour out your Spirit—sustaining and comforting—on these courageous truth-tellers, who demonstrate not only for themselves but for the millions of people who would lose access to affordable healthcare if this legislation were to pass.

Pour out your Spirit—revealing and convicting—on the senators who are so indifferent to the wellbeing of others.

Pour out your Spirit—leading and challenging—on those of us who feel powerless to stop this legislation, that we may not stop working for a better way. Amen.[76]

June 23, 2017

A friend requested that I pray for Robert Mueller, since it seems he has a large role to play in what happens next in the U.S. I have been hesitant to do so here, since I am praying for those who are resisting the current administration and the racism, sexism, and other forms of oppression it encourages. I have no idea if Mueller falls into this category, and—at best—his beliefs about such matters shouldn't influence the investigation. I don't want him to resist; I want him to find the truth. That's his task.

However, today I read a list of all the lies that have come from the White House since the inauguration. I watched the video of the shooting of Philando Castile. I saw photos of people with disabilities being dragged away from their wheelchairs for protesting a tax cut masquerading as a healthcare bill. Part of what we are resisting is the construction of a political discourse in which facts and accuracy are seen as irrelevant. The lack of truth is killing some of us already, and will be deadly for all of us soon enough.

---

76. Stein, "Disability advocates arrested during health care protest at McConnell's office."

Prayers

Please dear sweet baby Jesus, help Robert Mueller lead an investigation that finds truth, honors facts, and reports accurately. Amen.

June 24, 2017

God of Wisdom, bless the constituents of Republican Senator Dean Heller, who have communicated to him that his political career might end quickly if he supports a tax cut for the wealthy that is paid for by taking money from Medicaid. Amen.[77]

June 25, 2017

A prayer request from a wise friend:
God of Mercy, may Justice Anthony Kennedy continue to live a full and vibrant life, and continue to serve God and country and the common good as a Supreme Court justice. Amen.[78]

June 26, 2017

Enduring God, I pray tonight for the American Medical Association, the American Association of Retired Persons, the Catholic Health Association, and every other organization that is speaking out against the Senate's tax-cut-disguised-as-healthcare bill. Help us stand together for the common good. Amen.[79]

---

77. Martin and Burns, "Republican Senator vital to health bill's passage won't support it." Nevada Senator Dean Heller was seen as a "key swing vote" in the Republican healthcare bill. Republican proponents flooded local networks with TV ads and created the hashtag #HellerVotesYes to attempt to win his vote for the healthcare bill. In the end, Heller communicated that he wouldn't support it in its form due to the deep cuts to Medicaid and the voices of his constituents.

78. Johnson, "Kennedy stays quiet on whether he'll retire at end of Supreme Court term." Justice Anthony Kennedy is often the vote that determines the most controversial Supreme Court cases. Rumors began swirling in the late spring 2017 as to whether or not he would retire, since he is 80-years-old.

79. Japsen, "AMA says McConnell's Trumpcare bill violates 'do no harm' principle." On June 26, 2017, the largest association of doctors in the country, the American Medical Association, joined many of the nation's leading medical and advocacy groups voicing opposition to the latest version of the Repulican healthcare. In a letter written to Senate Majority Leader Mitch McConnell, the AMA's CEO, James Madra wrote "the draft legislation violates the *Primum non nocere* (first do no harm) standard on many levels."

Disciplined Hope

June 27, 2017

Faithful God, I pray for the six people who were arrested in Charleston, West Virginia, on Monday for demonstrating at Senator Shelley Moore Capito's office, asking her to vote against the Senate's tax-cut/healthcare bill. Their names are Rev. Jim Lewis, Kayla Parker, Joe Solomon, Bill Price, Terry Pickett, and Paul Dalzell. I am grateful for every person who protested, marched, made phone calls, or faxed representatives in the effort to stop this legislation. As these six were resisting in my beloved Mountain State, which has become deep red, I am particularly moved by their courage and witness. Bless them, dear God. Amen.[80]

June 28, 2017

God of Mercy, bless U.S. District Judge Mark Goldsmith, who issued a stay of removal for over 1,400 Iraqis living in the U.S. who are the focus of a mass deportation effort. Many are Christians who would be forcibly returned to areas in which Christians are persecuted. All would be sent into serious danger. May every act of compassion be multiplied. Amen.[81]

June 29, 2017

Holy God, bless every parent, grandparent, aunt, uncle, neighbor, teacher, babysitter, and friend who teaches children not to call names. Amen.

June 30, 2017

God of Hope, I give thanks for the officials from 25 states who have refused to comply or fully comply with the current administration's unwarranted

---

80. Zuckerman, "Six arrested in Capito's office after day of protesting health care bill." Half a dozen protestors were arrested Monday evening, June 26, 2017, outside Capito's office in Charleston, WV, saying that they wouldn't leave until Capito voted "no" on the proposed healthcare bill. Capito eventually did release a statement saying she would vote "no" on this version of the healthcare bill due to the "cuts to traditional Medicaid."

81. Chappell, "Federal judge temporarily blocks deportation of 1,400 Iraqis nationwide." The initial stay issued by U.S. District Judge Mark Goldsmith only protected 114 detainees from the Detroit area. However, lawyers from the ACLU filed an amended complaint that prevents ICE from deporting Iraqis from anywhere in the United States. The stay issued by Goldsmith halted the deportation all Iraqi nationals detained during immigration sweeps across the U.S. until at least July 10, 2017.

Prayers

request for a massive amount of voter information. Bless and protect them as they attempt to protect our democracy. Amen.[82]

July 1, 2017

Steadfast God, I pray tonight for every person who is remaining vigilant on a particular political issue as we resist the destructive rhetoric, actions, and policies of the current administration.

It feels like ethical whack-a-mole around here. A new cause for concern pops up every moment—more than any one person can address.

Help us all to find a way to raise our voices wherever needed without succumbing to distraction, dissolution, or despair. Amen.

July 2, 2017

Holy God, I give thanks for the former refugees, now in their 80s and 90s, who gathered in France last week to honor the man who helped them escape the Nazis. Aristides de Sousa Mendes was a Portuguese diplomat who defied government orders by granting visas to Jewish families fleeing persecution. The elders remembered his courage and asked for action to aid refugees today.

Bless the memory of Aristides de Sousa Mendes. Bless the former refugees who are advocating for current asylum seekers. Bless every person who contributes—in any way—to the well-being of those forced to flee their homes in search of peace and safety. Amen.[83]

---

82. Wines, "Asked for voters' data, states give Trump panel a bipartisan 'no.'" In a supposed investigation of voter fraud, Donald Trump asked for voter names, addresses, party affiliation, and voting records from all 50 states. Over 25 states refused to fully comply with the Presidential Advisory Commission on Election Integrity's request. White house spokesperson Sarah Huckabee Sanders called states' refusal to comply "a political stunt."

83. McAuley, "They were aided by Portugal's 'Schindler.' Now these WWII refugees are trying to help others." Numerous Jewish former refugees and their descendants gathered to acknowledge Aristides de Sousa Mendes's great sacrifice during WWII. Lissy Jarvik, of Dutch Jewish descent, fled to France following the invasion of the Netherlands. She states, "without Mendes, I would not be here. It's as simple as that."

Disciplined Hope

July 3, 2017

God of Grace, bless Hui Chen, who resigned from her position at the Department of Justice holding corporations accountable to ethics standards. Chen stated that the current administration engages in conduct that violates such standards, conduct that she would not tolerate in a company. She wanted no part in such hypocrisy.

Please surround Chen with grace. Grant that her message be heard. Ensure that her integrity is honored. Amen.[84]

July 4, 2017

God of Liberation, I give thanks for Dr. Bernice Johnson Reagon and Sweet Honey in the Rock for blessing us with Ella's Song. "We who believe in freedom cannot rest until it comes." Amen.[85]

July 5, 2017

God of Justice, bless Vanita Gupta, the CEO of the Leadership Conference on Civil and Human Rights. She is one of the many experts who see the current administration's requests for voter data, along with requests that election officials detail their compliance with the National Voter Registration Act of 1993, as a step towards large-scale voter suppression. May she be surrounded by colleagues in the work of justice. May her voice be heard and heeded. Amen.[86]

---

84. Zapotosky, "Justice Dept. compliance expert whose contract ended early says Trump conflicts made work feel hypocritical."

85. Ella's Song "is an anthem on the ultimate lesson of the freedom fight passed down generationally by Ms. Ella [Baker] herself that is meant to be spoken boldly out loud or under one's breath as the situation demands to empower both purpose and resolve. Her words set to voice and rhythm are a charge, a call to action wrapped in sonorous tones that harkens back as far as the slave days and forward to a new generation of equality, fairness, justice, and acceptance for everyone no matter what their origin." Online: https://ellabakercenter.org/blog/2013/12/ellas-song-we-who-believe-in-freedom-cannot-rest-until-it-comes.

86. Berman and Wagner, "Why almost every state is partially or fully rebuffing Trump's election commission." Vanita Gupta, former head of the Justice Department's civil rights division during the Obama administration, said, "There's going to be a whole problem of uniformity and consistency that could create a lot of problems, even with the compiling of publicly available data," when commenting on Donald Trump's request for voter data, "It's hugely problematic to do this kind of thing and to do it with at least no

Prayers

July 6, 2017

Creator God, I pray tonight for the U.S. Court of Appeals for the District of Columbia Circuit, which ruled against the current administration's efforts to suspend an Obama-era rule restricting methane emissions from new oil and gas wells.

Grant sacred power to all who care for and protect the Earth. Amen.[87]

July 7, 2017

God of Abundance, I lift up all those who love across boundaries and bloodlines and borders. Due to the partial implementation of the current administration's travel ban targeting Muslims, the government is drawing limitations on what is recognized as close family. This seems nonsensical to me (and not just because grandparents are excluded). Love makes family, and love doesn't work that way.

Help us to love each other fiercely in these days. Amen.

July 8, 2017

God of Grace, bless Pete Souza, the White House photographer during President Obama's tenure. His timely posts of old photos serve as a consistent reminder that what is happening now is neither normal nor acceptable. Please continue to inspire him. Amen.

July 9, 2017

Fierce God of Love and Power, I give thanks for the Catholic sisters who are dedicating an open-air chapel on their land in Pennsylvania in the path of the proposed Atlantic Sunrise pipeline. Their order, the Adorers of the Blood of Christ, owns the land, but the legal intricacies of eminent domain

---

explicit regard for existing privacy laws and concerns and no explicit mention of how this data will be used."

87. Friedman, "Court blocks E.P.A. effort to suspend Obama-era methane rule." The decision from the U.S. Court of Appeals for the District of Columbia Circuit was a "setback" for Scott Pruitt, the EPA administrator who spent much of his time in 2017 dismantling numerous Obama-era environmental regulations.

Disciplined Hope

allow the Williams Partners to build and operate a pipeline through it. The sisters say this pipeline would violate their faith and their land ethic.

May their witness be powerful and their influence wide. Bless them with your joyful Presence. Amen.[88]

July 10, 2017

God of Mercy, I was awed today by the determined humanity of beachgoers in Florida who clasped hands and locked arms to save a family caught in a riptide. Several individuals had tried to rescue the swimmers, but they were also caught in the current. Then the people on the beach formed a human chain and accomplished together what no one could do alone.

Theologian Marion Grau pointed out that health insurance works on the same principle.

Bless everyone trying to make a human chain to help those caught in the tide. Amen.[89]

July 12, 2017

God of Wisdom, I pray for guidance for all of us who care for this country as a terribly flawed but hopeful experiment in democratic governance.

For some of us, the election of the current resident of the White House was unimaginable, because his behavior runs afoul of social and political norms. His actions since the inauguration have been similar—disregard and disdain for basic manners, honesty, decency, integrity, governmental protocol, and the noblest values of our country.

---

88. Zuazmer, "Catholic nuns in Pa. build a chapel to block the path of a gas pipeline planned for their property." Catholic nuns in Pennsylvania resisted the $3 billion fracking gas pipeline by creating an open-air chapel in the middle of a cornfield, launching a legal battle and citing religious freedom. The pipeline "goes against everything we believe in—we believe in the sustenance of all creation," Sister Linda Fischer reported.

89. Mettler, "Rip currents swept away a Florida family. Then beachgoers formed a human chain." Roberta Ursrey was enjoying a family vacation at Panama City Beach when she noticed that her sons were too far from the shore. She and other relatives tried to swim to them, but they all became trapped in a rip current. Nine people total were trapped in 15 feet of water. Over 30 people linked arms to tow the Ursrey family safely to shore.

Prayers

For others, the election of President Barack Obama was unimaginable because it ran afoul of one of the most deeply entrenched social and political norms in America: those in power are expected to be white.

Right now we, as a nation, are deciding which of these social and political norms we wish to hand on to our children. Help us, God. Amen.

July 13, 2017

Creator God, bless the Sri Lankan Navy, which rescued an elephant caught in a riptide. Elephants are excellent swimmers, but currents are fierce. It took four vessels and a team of divers to get the elephant to solid ground.

It feels like the U.S. is caught in a political and cultural riptide. Learning from the examples of the family in Florida and the elephant in Sri Lanka, it seems the way to escape a riptide is sustained collective effort, backed by the communal will to care for our fellows.

Help us, oh God, to swim together and to guide one another to shore. Amen.[90]

July 14, 2017

Holy God, I pray for the senators who plan to vote against the GOP's Medicaid-cutting healthcare bill. I pray for those senators who are undecided. Grant them strength. Give them guidance. Call them toward the common good. Amen.[91]

July 15, 2017

God of Compassion, I pray for John Kasich, Governor of Ohio, who repudiated false claims about Medicaid from the White House. Bless all governors who are looking out for the well-being of their constituents. Amen.[92]

---

90. Horton, "An elephant was stranded nine miles out to sea. Then the Sri Lankan Navy arrived."

91. Pear and Kaplan, "Senate Republicans unveil new health bill, but divisions remain."

92. Sullivan, Eilperin, and Balz, "White House lauches aggressive push to flip GOP governors opposed to Senate health bill."

Disciplined Hope

July 16, 2017

God of Grace, I pray blessing on all the different groups from various religious organizations in Louisville who are holding prayer vigils around the city in solidarity with immigrant neighbors. They are drawing attention to the increasing deportations and detentions that are harming our community.

One of the primary tasks of a Christian is to not look away from suffering. This is too enormous for any one of us to pull it off alone. We can only bear to witness the reality of suffering (and of grace) together, each doing what we can when we can. We tag-team, relay, and rally our way through.

Those holding vigil remind us that we are in this together, and we must care for all. Amen.

July 17, 2017

Holy God, bless the senators who oppose the GOP-proposed Medicaid-cutting "healthcare" legislation. Thank you. Amen.[93]

July 18, 2017

God of Revelation, we don't know what heaven will be like, because we cannot fathom your glory. Some days, though, I imagine it will be like this: Jane Austen has been writing novels since she died, and when I die I get to read them all.

This is not my most intricate theological take on beatific vision. But it isn't entirely foolish, either.

There is something holy in precise and illuminating use of language. There is grace in seeing straight through human pretensions and still hoping things turn out right in the end.

Jane Austen, through her writing, resisted sexism, classism, and idiocy. Her novels are still a rebellion today, because they testify to the power

---

93. Kaplan, "Health care overhaul collapses as two Republican Senators defect." Two more Republican senators, Mike Lee of Utah and Jerry Moran of Kansas, declared that they opposed the Senate Republican bill to repeal the Affordable Care Act. This version of the GOP healthcare legislation would cut medicaid funding without offering a suitable replacement. With four Republican votes against the bill, leaders were forced to let this version of the healthcare bill die.

of language to reveal truth. Of course I never met Mrs. Norris. But when I read about her I gasped in recognition.

I give thanks for Jane Austen, who died 200 years ago today. Amen.

July 19, 2017

Merciful God, I lift in prayer everyone who is struggling with health issues. May each and every person have excellent medical care. Amen.

July 20, 2017

God of Compassion, I pray for the ArchCity Defenders, a civil rights law firm in St. Louis that fights abuses of legal systems, including keeping poor people in jail for being poor. There is a dangerous heat wave in Missouri and there are people being held in vermin-infested medium-security jail with no air conditioning. The facility is called the Workhouse. Today, the ArchCity Defenders offered to bail out anyone kept in the Workhouse due to lack of funds.

God, I give thanks for this powerful witness to compassion and human dignity. Bless each employee of this firm. Knowing some little bit of the work they have been doing, I suspect they are tired, underpaid, daily faced with tragedy, and hauling uphill. I ask that you grant them restorative and healing rest. Unexpected funding sources. Breathtaking experiences of beauty, kindness, renewal, and love. And an easing of burdens as the Spirit moves with them in all they do. Amen.[94]

---

94. Seventy percent of the 770 inmates of St. Louis's medium security jail known as the "Workhouse" are housed in the non-air-conditioned portion of the building. During the week of July 17, 2017, temperatures in Missouri reached triple digits. The ArchCity Defenders stated that it is not a humane place for anyone to live in and so they decided it was time to intervene and do something. If not in time for this heat wave, then maybe the next. On July 21, 2017, they were able to bail 15 people out of jail and they continue to raise money for the cause. To learn more or to donate, go to https://www.generosity.com/community-fundraising/beyond-bail-fund-2017.

Disciplined Hope

July 21, 2017

Holy God, bless Ksenija Pavlovic, who resisted the administration's ongoing restrictions of the press by live-streaming the audio of a White House press briefing. Amen.[95]

July 27, 2017

God of Presence, I pray for the doctors, nurses, staff, volunteers, and escorts at Planned Parenthood locations and women's health clinics. Many are being harassed and threatened. Set a hedge against all evil to protect them and their families. Help this country to move towards accessible and affordable healthcare for all. Amen.[96]

July 28, 2017

God of Justice, the rule of law is threatened profoundly by the current occupant of the White House, who seeks loyalty and privilege rather than truth or the common good. Tonight I give thanks for Aeschylus, who wrote a trilogy of plays that are known as the Oresteia. One of the themes of the drama is the transition from vengeance to justice through trials. The Oresteia was performed to great critical acclaim in Athens in 458 BCE.

Many recent events make me feel as if the U.S. is going back in time, to eras in which racism, sexism, and heterosexism were openly proclaimed and approved. Aeschylus reminds me that human brokenness (my words, not his) exists in every time and place. What fairness we manage has always required artists and prophets to spur outrage, thinkers and planners to create systems that hedge against our worst tendencies, and engaged citizens to live out norms of equity. Bless all who aim to fill these roles today. Amen.

---

95. Borchers, "A reporter broke White House rules by streaming live audio of an off-camera briefing." White House news briefings have been chaotic, irregular, and limited since the Trump administration took office. For a time, reporters were not allowed to use audio- or video-recording equipment—a major change in protocol from prior administrations. Pavlovic, a former political science teaching fellow at Yale, started her own news site, Pavlovic Today, and appointed herself the White House correspondent in order to stream audio of the briefings by Sarah Huckabee Sanders.

96. To learn more about Planned Parenthood, go to https://www.plannedparenthood.org.

Prayers

July 29, 2017

Holy God, I pray for those taking the Presbyterian Church (USA) ordination exams this week. After years of study, those seeking ordination take difficult and exhausting exams so that, if they pass, they can apply for scarce, demanding jobs that don't pay well. If successful in this process, they will spend their lives in spaces of struggle and suffering, accompanying those who are lost or have lost or are set up to lose.

Seminary students are, by many standards, batshit crazy. Misfits and whackadoos. I see your presence in their persistence. Their commitment to love God and neighbor sustains my hope. I am awed and honored to learn with them.

Help them during these arduous exams. Grant them clarity of thought, quickness of recall, focus, and blessed writing skills. Amen.

July 30, 2017

Holy God, I pray for every law enforcement organization and officer who has spoken out against the Occupant's endorsement of police brutality. It is not enough to say the right thing. More is needed, including serious reform that addresses racial bias in policing.

However, one of the lessons of our current era is that when saying the wrong thing becomes socially acceptable, hateful actions rise.

May justice and kindness be always on our lips; may we enact mercy and compassion. Amen.

July 31, 2017

Steadfast God, bless those who work for, are members of, or support the American Civil Liberties Union. Grant them success in their persistent efforts to protect the vulnerable and uphold the rule of law. Amen.[97]

---

97. To learn more about the ACLU, go to https://www.aclu.org.

Disciplined Hope

August 1, 2017

God of Strength, bless Adm. Paul F. Zukunft, head of the Coast Guard, who said he will "not turn [his] back" on and "will not break faith" with transgender service members in the Coast Guard. Amen.[98]

August 2, 2017

God of Love, bless Governor Kate Brown and the state legislature of Oregon as they work to expand healthcare access, protect state forests, and fight discrimination. Amen.[99]

August 3, 2017

God of Grace, bless Elizabeth Southerland, an EPA official who resigned in protest of the current administration's rejection of facts and refusal to address environmental dangers. Amen.[100]

August 4, 2017

Eternal God, I give thanks for friends who do not drift away with time and distance. In a culture of short memories, long-time friendships are a source

---

98. Nixon, "Coast Guard still supports transgender troops, commandant says." Gibbons-Neff, "Despite Trump announcement, Coast Guard will not." The commandant of the Coast Guard, Paul F. Zunkunft, reported on August 1, 2017, that he would continue to encourage and support transgender troops even in light of Donald Trump's tweets saying that the government would not allow transgender individuals to serve in the military.

99. Somashekhar, "Oregon approves sweeping bill expanding abortion access." Oregon governor Kate Brown declared a state of emergency on August 2, 2017, due to the amount of wildfire activity throughout the state. The record-breaking heat wave that swept across the Pacific Northwest made the threat of wildfires higher. At the same time, Brown and the state legislature looked to expand Medicaid funding and birth-control access as the administration attempted to decrease funding and access to both.

100. Davidson, "EPA won't be able to do the right thing under Trump, says latest protesting official." Senior U.S. Official Elizabeth Sutherland resigned her post on August 1, 2017, reporting that the Trump administration has led to "the temporary triumph of myth over truth." Sutherland received the Presidential Rank Award of Distinguished Executive in 2015, but says that it all changed when Administrator Scott Pruitt took over. Planned rollbacks of environmental regulations and funding cuts are some of the reasons Sutherland listed for her resignation in her exit memo.

Prayers

of grounding and a reminder of the value of faithfulness. I am grateful. Amen.

August 5, 2017

Holy God, I lift up the members of the grand jury impaneled by special counsel Robert Mueller. May they both seek the truth and find it. Amen.[101]

August 6, 2017

God of Strength, bless the city of Chicago, which is suing the current administration over Jeff Sessions's threats to withhold public safety grant money from sanctuary cities. Chicago is standing up for immigrants, police officers, and the common good. Pour your Spirit on this city, dear God. Amen.[102]

August 7, 2017

God of Compassion, I pray for all who long for a better world. Our yearning is a form of faith. Don't leave us on our own. Amen.

August 8, 2017

God of Peace, it is an anxious day. The insanity of war looms.

---

101. Leonnig, Horwitz, and Zapotosky, "Special Counsel Mueller using grand jury in federal court in Washington as part of Russia investigation." A grand jury was established in Washington in order to pursue evidence of collusion with the Kremlin. In the U.S. legal system, a grand jury has the power to issue subpoenas and ultimately indictments at the request of the prosecutors. Mueller's investigation has been using a sitting grand jury in Virginia to authorize documents and witnesses, but the addition of a separate grand jury in Washington suggests that Mueller and his team will be making extensive use of it going forward in the investigation.

102. Somashekhar, "Chicago sues Justice Department over new police grant rules targeting Sanctuary Cities." The city of Chicago sued U.S. Attorney General Jeff Sessions over his threat to withhold federal funding from cities that don't cooperate with the Trump administration's crackdown on undocumented immigrants. According to the complaint filed by the city of Chicago, the new conditions, "fly in the face of a longstanding city policy that promotes cooperation between local law enforcement and immigrant communities."

Disciplined Hope

I pray for every person who thinks carefully about the best ways to keep soldiers and civilians safe. In particular, I lift up Senator Tammy Duckworth, a veteran who was awarded the Purple Heart after losing her legs while serving in Iraq. Duckworth is fighting the Occupant's nomination of Steven Bradbury to a post in the administration. Bradbury was a Justice Department lawyer who authored the "torture memos" that authorized waterboarding and other torture techniques. Duckworth argues that—in addition to all the other reasons torture is wrong—torturing prisoners put U.S. soldiers in greater danger.

The perils of war include not only injury and death, but dehumanization. Bless all who hold on to that which is humane. Amen.[103]

August 9, 2017

God of Hope and Anger, bless the residents of Ferguson, MO, who protested the killing of Mike Brown. Amen.[104]

August 10, 2017

God of Determination, I pray tonight for the Homrich 9. Activists in Detroit, in 2014 they blocked trucks from shutting off the water of citizens who could not pay exorbitant rates.

More than 40 percent of Detroit residents live below the poverty line. In 2014, the city cut off the water supply to thousands of vulnerable citizens—including many children, elders, and people with disabilities—who were three months late or $150 short on their payments. The city spent more on these shut-offs than it would have cost to implement an affordability plan that would have prevented shut-offs and increased municipal

---

103. Savage, "Trump nominee who wrote Bush-era torture memo is scrutinized." Former George W. Bush administration official Steven Bradbury wrote legal memos authorizing the use of torture by the CIA. In early June, Donald Trump nominated him to be his general counsel for the Transportation Department. On July 29, 2017, Tammy Duckworth, a veteran whose helicopter was shot down behind enemy lines, led the protest against this nomination stating that Bradbury "lacked the judgment to stand up and say what is morally right."

104. Buchanan, "What happened in Ferguson?" August 9, 2017, marked the third anniversary of the killing of Mike Brown. Dozens of people gathered to rebuild the makeshift memorial that still stands, marking the location of the death of an unarmed black teenager by a white police officer.

revenue. Because the city had been put under emergency management in 2013, the people of Detroit could not use their voting power to change things.

With no legal or governmental recourse available, people linked arms and bodily blocked the gates at the Homrich Company, the private company that performed the shut offs.

Nine were arrested. During a trial, the jury appeared to understand this act of civil disobedience. The trial was halted to prevent the activists from being heralded as heroes. Later, the nine were let off on a technicality nearly three years after their arrest. Their actions slowed the water shut-offs and brought attention, and some relief, but not a complete resolution of the problem.

Tonight, while current events make every moment seem particularly volatile, I am grateful for those brave souls who are in this justice work for the long haul. The Homrich 9 were impatient with injustice and yet radically patient in their commitment to the common good.

Help us, God, to know when impatience is called for and when patience is needed. Help us to keep working even when there is no easy answer or quick fix. Help us to know when to link arms and stand together. Amen.[105]

August 12, 2017

Holy God, I stand in awe of the mighty faithfulness of the counter protestors in Charlottesville today. Please pour out blessing on each and every one. Grant healing, rest, and kindness. May their witness reverberate, growing in power. And help the rest of us further their efforts to confront and reject white nationalism. Amen.[106]

---

105. Candace, "Trial dismissed against 'Homrich 9' water protestors."

106. Stolberg and Rosenthal, "Man charged after white nationalist rally in Charlottesville ends in deadly violence." The governor of Virginia declared a state of emergency in Charlottesville, VA, on Saturday, August 12, 2017, as white nationalists fought with counter protestors over an attempt to remove a Confederate general statue from a city park. The clash turned deadly when a speeding car slammed into the counter protestors, killing one and injuring nineteen.

Disciplined Hope

August 13, 2017

Mighty God, I lift up every person who went to a march, vigil, rally, or other type of gathering to stand against white nationalism. There are more Nazis in the U.S. than I realized. But there are also more people of good will who will not go quietly. Grant us strength, courage, stubbornness, and loud voices. Amen.

August 14, 2017

Holy God, bless the people of Durham, North Carolina, who pulled down a Confederate statue today. Amen.[107]

August 15, 2017

Dear God, please help us. Pour out on us a Spirit of logic, reason, coherence, and honesty. Strengthen all who resist double-talk, self-deception, and the demonic power of white nationalism. Amen.

August 16, 2017

God of Multitudes, there are many people resisting the Occupant's false equivalences that serve to encourage and condone white nationalism. I give thanks for each and every one. Every tiny bit counts.

In particular, tonight I lift up the city of Baltimore. The city council voted to remove Confederate statues. They were taken down in the night. Done. The work is not over in Baltimore, by any means, but I am encouraged by this efficiency.

Please God, may our nation as a whole reject and remove prominent Nazi sympathizers with similar alacrity. Amen.[108]

---

107. Astor, "Protestors in Durham topple a Confederate monument." A protest in downtown Durham, NC, on Monday, August 14, 2017, left a Confederate Soldiers Monument in pieces on the ground. The monument stood in front of the old Durham County Courthouse and was pulled down to show solidarity with anti-racist activists after the deadly clashes in Charlottesville, VA.

108. Bidgood, Fandos, and Goldman, "Baltimore Mayor Had Statues Removed in 'Best Interest of My City.'" The city of Baltimore, MD removed all four of its Confederate statues in the middle of the night on Tuesday, August 15, 2017. This occurred between 11:30 p.m. and 5:30 a.m. one day after the removal was approved by the city council.

Prayers

August 17, 2017

God of Hope, bless the many activists who attempted to surrender for toppling a Confederate statue earlier this week. Photographs of the long line of people outside the courthouse in Durham County give me hope.

Let your Spirit breathe through and among us, dear God, conspiring for a better world. Amen.

August 18, 2017

Creator God, bless the former members of the President's Committee on the Arts and the Humanities. They resigned today with purpose and panache, and called on the Occupant to resign also. From their mouths to your ear, oh God. Amen.[109]

August 19, 2017

God bless Boston.
And Pikeville, Kentucky.
And every city and town across the country where white nationalists showed up to scare people and found themselves outnumbered. Amen.[110]

Mayor Catherine Pugh is quoted saying, "I do not want to endanger people in my own city" and therefore chose to "move quickly."

109. Pogrebin, "Sixteen members of White House Arts Committee resign to protest Trump." Members of the President's Arts and Humanities Committee submitted a joint letter of resignation directed to the President stating, "We cannot sit idly by, the way that your West Wing advisors have, without speaking out against your words and actions." The first letter of each paragraph of the letter spelled out "Resist."

110. Etman, "Thousands counter-protest 'Free Speech' Rally in Boston." Over 40,000 counter-protestors showed up to oppose a scheduled "free speech" rally by white supremacist groups in Boston. By 11:00 a.m. on Saturday, August 19, 2017, the counter-protestors outnumbered those present for the "free speech" rally. A similar situation happened in Pikeville, KY, when Neo-Nazis faced counter protests from an Antifa (anti-fascist) group during their White Power Rally.

Disciplined Hope

August 20, 2017

Steadfast God, I pray for those who work for and support the Southern Poverty Law Center, which has been fighting hate for decades. Overwhelm them with success. Amen.[111]

August 21, 2017

God of Heaven and Earth, thank you for this day. Experiencing wonder is fundamentally humanizing. Sharing awe with strangers is profoundly life-affirming.

Thank you for the intricate, bodacious beauty of the universe.

Bless the scientists who help us know when, where, and how to see the glory of creation. Amen.[112]

August 22, 2017

God of Grace, I lift up all the people who don't decide to be activists, they just can't help it. People who do not ponder how to intervene when Archibald makes a racist comment, because the words "racist nonsense" are already out of their mouths before Archie gets to the punctuation. People whose shelves are filled with books written by authors of every imaginable background. People who are so fundamentally fair-minded that they could no more choose to ignore injustice than they could choose to disobey the laws of gravity.

Bless them, God. Grant the rest of us—those of us who have to think about it and work up the nerve—a portion of that unselfconscious courage. Amen.

---

111. To learn more about the Southern Poverty Law Center, see https://www.splcenter.org.

112. Fountain, "At total solar eclipse leaves a nation in awe." On August 21 there was a solar eclipse. The path of totality crossed the United States, allowing millions to experience the event.

Prayers

August 23, 2017

Holy God, bless Colin Kaepernick in his powerful witness against racism in the United States. Bless those who join him and bless those who stand in solidarity with him. Amen.[113]

August 24, 2017

Creator God, I lift up Daniel Kammen, formerly the State Department Science Envoy. Kammen resigned in protest of the Occupant's policies and rhetoric. The first letters of each paragraph in his resignation letter spell out "impeach."

Open doors of opportunity for Kammen to work for energy sustainability and ecological responsibility. Let his leadership in international scientific cooperation be a powerful force for the healing of our environment and the flourishing of all people. Amen.[114]

August 26, 2017

God of Justice and Love, I give thanks for the faithful witness of Catholic Worker communities. Grant them a palpable sense of your abundant grace; sustain them with joy and delight. Amen.[115]

---

113. Belson, "Kaepernick's protest cascades into protests over his job situation." 49ers quarterback Colin Kaepernick refused to stand for the national anthem to protest police brutality on August 26, 2016. Since then, he has not been signed by any other NFL team. Almost one year later, on August 23, 2017, more than 1,000 people crowded outside the NFL's Manhattan offices wearing Kaepernick jerseys to protest the discrimination he is facing surrounding exercising his free-speech rights.

114. Wang, "Trump's science envoy quits in scathing letter with an embedded message: I-M-P-E-A-C-H." Daniel Kammen, an energy professor at the University of California, Berkeley, was appointed to the position of the State Department's science envoy in February of 2016. On Wednesday, August 23, 2017, he resigned from this position, saying that his decision was tied to Trump's "attacks on core values of the United States."

115. To learn more about the Catholic Worker movement, see https://www.catholicworker.org.

Disciplined Hope

August 26, 2017

God, we need to talk. Marilyn McCord Adams, who knew you better than anyone else I've ever met in my whole life, said the faithful thing to do was to be like the Psalmist and take my problems straight to the top. So here are a few things about which I am concerned:

1. There is a category 4 hurricane bearing down on Texas, while we have a science-hating dingbat in charge.
2. Above-mentioned dingbat pardoned Joe Arpaio, a criminal racist who targeted and tortured people of color. This exemplifies the Occupant's incredible contempt for our judicial system, communicates to his white-nationalist base that black and brown people can be harmed with impunity, and stokes racial conflict.
3. North Korea is launching missiles. WTF?
4. The Occupant's threatened economic craziness with both the debt ceiling and the Federal Reserve puts the global economy in danger. GLOBAL.
5. The Coward in Chief is also targeting transgender military personnel, because he has enough hate to spread it around.
6. Right in here we could use some smart people in the State Department and other areas of government. However, racist dingbat coward appointed a few unqualified millionaires and left a lot of positions empty. So we are lacking, say, people who could prevent war.
7. But at least our election process has been hacked by Russians and we fall for tweets by Russian bots. 'Cause we are THAT smart.

God, we need some HELP in here. We clearly cannot manage this on our own. There are good people trying but we need ASSISTANCE.

Also, I am really, really pissed that Marilyn McCord Adams died. Amen.[116]

---

[116]. Adams, "Marilyn McCord Adams obituary." Rev. Dr. Marilyn McCord Adams was a theologian, philosopher, and priest whose academic work focused on the problem of evil. She died on March 22, 2017.

Prayers

August 27, 2017

Holy God, I pray for the thousands of heroes today who helped those affected by hurricane Harvey. I give thanks for the acts of kindness, of neighbors helping neighbors, strangers lending hands, first responders working tirelessly, nurses and others looking out not only for themselves but for those in their care. We will never know all the acts of bravery and valor, compassion and benevolence. But you see and know and honor every act of good will.

In the coming days, let the circle of solidarity expand, such that each and every one of us finds some way to assist those in the path of the storm.

And God, please stop the rain. Weather is natural; climate change is our own damn fault. Tip the scales in our favor anyway, out of your own mercy. Scatter the clouds, please Jesus. Amen.[117]

August 27, 2017

Merciful God, protect the people of Texas. Save them from the rushing waters. Protect the pets and farm animals, the wildlife and the vegetation, the habitats and landscapes.

Bless all Texans with a spirit of solidarity that they may come together in this crisis and care for one another. Help those of us not in Texas support them with vigilant prayer and financial contributions.

We know, God, that we humans have harmed our environment so that storms are worsened. In your divine compassion, calm the winds, scatter the clouds, and stop the rain. Amen.

August 28, 2017

Holy God, bless those who participated in the Ministers March for Justice in Washington DC today. Leaders from different faith traditions were united in their call for civil rights and social justice. May their combined voices be heard and their call heeded. Amen.[118]

---

117. Cirillo, "Harvey brings catastrophic floods to Houston; at least five reported dead." The end of August 2017 brought devastating and record-breaking flooding to towns across Texas from Hurricane Harvey.

118. Stein and Zauzmer, "Dueling clergy protests over the Trump presidency converge on Washington." Ministers, rabbis, imams, and their congregants marched together

Disciplined Hope

August 29, 2017

Merciful God, I pray for the attorney general of Illinois, Lisa Madigan, who filed a lawsuit to push for police reform in Chicago. The Justice Department investigated policing practices in Chicago and found a pattern of excessive force. Normally, this would lead to an agreement for changes that could be enforced by the courts. The Occupant and Jeff Sessions put a stop to this process. Attorney General Madigan is trying to go forward towards reform anyway.

Bless her with stubbornness, with colleagues in the fight, with support along the way, and with positive, structural improvements in Chicago policing. Amen.[119]

August 30, 2017

God of Refuge, bless U.S. District Judge Orlando Garcia, who blocked the implementation of a law in Texas designed to punish sanctuary cities and increase deportations. Garcia hails from San Antonio.

As far as I can tell, the random guys with boats who showed up in Houston aren't asking about immigration status before they rescue people from the floodwaters. Neither are the thousands of volunteers working night and day to provide shelter, food, water, medical services, diapers, and everything else that is needed. There is immeasurable wisdom in their indiscriminate care.

God bless Texas. Amen.[120]

---

on the National Mall on Monday, August 28, 2017, to protest Donald Trump's administration as well as to recommit to the principles of Dr. Martin Luther King Jr. The One Thousand Ministers March for Justice was intentionally convened on the anniversary of King's "I Have a Dream" speech.

119. Smith, "Illinois Attorney General sues Chicago over police practices." Illinois attorney general Lisa Madigan sued the city of Chicago on Tuesday, August 29, 2017 stating that Mayor Rahm Emanuel's reforms are not sufficient to prevent the Chicago police department from continuing a pattern of deadly and excessive force that disproportionately targets African-Americans and Latinos.

120. Fernandez, "Federal judge blocks Texas' ban on 'Sanctuary Cities.'" On Wednesday, August 30, 2017, a federal district judge ruled against the state of Texas and halted major provisions of a controversial state-based immigration enforcement law. This bill was one of Governor Greg Abbott's legislative priorities that seek to outlaw "sanctuary" entities.

Prayers

September 1, 2017

God of Hope, bless Representative Ruben Kihuen and Repesenative Adriano Espaillat. As members of congress who came to the U.S. as undocumented immigrants, Kihuen and Espaillat urged the Occupant to extend the Deferred Action for Childhood Arrivals. DACA was put in place to allow people who were brought to the U.S. as undocumented, immigrant children—called Dreamers—to live and work in this country legally and without the constant fear of deportation. These protections are under threat. Rule-abiding, tax-paying, beloved neighbors are anxious and afraid.

Pour out your blessings on the Dreamers, God. May they shape a vision of what the United States could be—a place of opportunity, equality, and hope—that guides our aspirations. Make a way out of no way, God.

Sustain, inspire, and empower those who are advocating for Dreamers in congress and everywhere else. Amen.[121]

September 2, 2017

Holy God, bless Representative Jeff Jackson, who is leading the charge against gerrymandering in North Carolina. May justice and honesty prevail. Amen.[122]

---

121. Weigel, "Immigrant members of Congress ask Trump to keep DACA." The end of August and beginning of September 2017 saw Donald Trump thinking through the end of DACA, a program that protects undocumented immigrants who came to the U.S. as children. Two congressmen, Representatives Rubén Kihuen and Adriano Espaillat, who were also once undocumented have attempted to appeal to the president to keep the program. There are an estimated 800,000 Dreamers across the U.S. Many sources reported on August 31, 2017, that the president was expected to end the program, even though an official statement had not been made.

122. Bullock, "Gerrymandering and recruiting: A candidate ME conversation with Sen. Jackson." At 35 years old, Jeff Jackson is one of the youngest senators. He won the seat while living in Charlotte, North Carolina, but once he go to the Senate, he realized he would have virtually no influence in shaping legislation. The district lines, drawn by the lawmakers themselves, were so gerrymandered that few seats had competitive general elections, meaning that the legislature's tone was decided in the GOP primaries. Jackson uses the example of House Bill 2, which banned many transgender people from using the appropriate restrooms in public, to show how certain bills can be passed or kept in place by gerrymandering. Jackson is now one of many working for the elimination of gerrymandering.

Disciplined Hope

September 3, 2017

Faithful God, I pray for the Anne Frank Center for Mutual Respect, a Jewish organization that counters prejudice and discrimination while advocating for kindness and fairness. Amen.[123]

September 4, 2017

God of Wisdom, I pray for every college and university administrator, every professor and teacher and counselor, who is staying up late to figure out how to protect students who are Dreamers. Help them to be sharp and clever. Give them resourcefulness, ingenuity, determination, and cunning. Amen.[124]

September 5, 2017

Holy God, today has been a day of intercessory prayer. I have lifted up to you sons and mothers, children and friends. Tonight, I lift up people in a different way, honoring them and asking for your blessing on their resistance.

I saw this group of people outside Mitch McConnell's office in Louisville, KY, but I know that similar groups—actually, members of the same group!—met in towns and cities across the U.S. They gathered to protest the Occupant's move to rescind DACA. . . . And they were beautiful.

They were an awkward and clumsy lot. The few with poise and elegance were not enough to elevate the whole. Most of us arrived with a friend and then got shuffled into an amorphous mass as we tried to let people through. The 20-something hipster in skinny jeans stood next to the 40-something man wearing a fanny pack unironically. The guy with full-sleeve tattoos handed the microphone to a gentleman in his 80s bringing a message from "the older generation." I don't know what the message was, exactly, since

---

123. "Our mission is to honor the legacy of Anne Frank and the continuing relevance of *Anne Frank: The Diary of a Young Girl*. Central to our mission, the Anne Frank Center for Mutual Respect offers educational programs, traveling exhibits, theatrical performances, and annual scholarships to bring her message to new generations and honor those inspired to humanitarian action through her words." For more information, see https://www.annefrank.com/

124. Adams and Hoisington, "What major univerisites had to say about Trump's move to roll back DACA."

no one held the mic close enough to their mouths and we only heard every third word. A lady with lovely white hair had to leave early, so she offered her handmade "I support DACA" sign to a young black man when she left. He later passed it on to a man who I'm guessing is originally from Central America, and who could make a living as a supermodel. I tried not to stare.

A young woman who is a DACA recipient spoke of her anxiety. When she finished speaking, six or seven Latina women joined arms with her, shoulder to shoulder.

A great guy I know from church played a drum, which was almost enough to keep us chanting in rhythm. An Indian mother had her child in a stroller. Like many of the other children present, the kiddo seemed completely accustomed to demonstrations.

Some signs were newly made for the occasion, but many had clearly seen heavy use already. The people holding them had turned out to protest the Muslim ban, police brutality, and 14 other manifestations of white supremacy in the past few years.

One man looked so much like my family back home that I asked him if he was originally from West Virginia. He said no, but I'm sure we're kin.

Among the English chants with poor meter and the Spanish chants I couldn't understand, there was this statement, shouted fiercely by the crowd, that seemed a North star of truth: "If you come for one of us, you come for all of us."

May it be so. Amen.[125]

September 6, 2017

God of Faithfulness, I pray again for Robert Mueller. In the midst of daily chaos and weekly insanity, may he continue his investigations with integrity, honesty, discipline, and all due haste. Set a hedge around him to protect him from all evil. Surround him with intelligent colleagues who are committed to the common good. Defend him from deceitfulness of every kind. Amen.

---

125. McDonogh, "DACA supporters rally at federal courthouse after order rescinded." Donald Trump announced on September 5, 2017, that he would rescind the Deferred Action for Childhood Arrivals program. This announcement sparked numerous protests across the country similar to the one described in Louisville, KY, in order to show support for the 800,000 affected.

Disciplined Hope

September 7, 2017

Holy God, bless Ta-Nehisi Coates. Telling the truth is, in itself, an exercise of hope. May he continue to write in fierce faithfulness to truth and profound rejection of deception. Amen.[126]

September 8, 2017

Merciful God, I pray for the 16 attorneys general who are suing to prevent the current administration from ending DACA. The suit notes that rescinding the program—even though DACA is vastly beneficial in human and economic terms—is of a piece with the Occupant's anti-Mexican prejudice and rhetoric.

Bless these public servants with clear thinking, cogent arguments, a fair hearing, and victory. Amen.[127]

September 9, 2017

Holy God, I lift up every scientist—climatologist, meteorologist, geographer, oceanographer, and all the others, too—whose work helps us understand and track weather events. Every bit of advance notice saves lives. Bless them. Amen.

September 10, 2017

God of Peace, I lift up The Salaam Network in Louisville, which offers education about Islam, about Abrahamic religions, and about values that are commonly held among many religions.

The goals of TSN—communal peace and wholeness in which religious differences are recognized and respected—are lofty. And no one working for the organization is making a dime. These are volunteers with other commitments trying to change the world after the kids are in bed, retirees

---

126. Ta-Nehisi Coates is an author who has written insightfully about race in the United States and about the presidency of Donald Trump. To learn more, see: http://ta-nehisicoates.com

127. The Associated Press, "Sixteen Attorneys General sue Trump administration over ending DACA."

Prayers

who've basically gone back to work for free, and middle-aged people of good will giving up their weekends.

I think they might pull it off. Amen.[128]

September 11, 2017

Creator God, bless Pope Francis in his ongoing efforts to emphasize care of the earth as a vital aspect of Christian faith. He does not have patience for those who claim climate change is a theory or a "hoax." Yesterday he spoke of the moral responsibility that we all share to care for the environment. May we have eyes to see and ears to hear the truths set before us. And may each person who has a position of influence use it to protect our common home. Amen.[129]

September 12, 2017

God of Love, I give thanks for the life and witness of Edith Windsor, who fought and won a legal battle against the Defense of Marriage Act and who died today. As she enters into eternal rejoicing, may she be welcomed by love, love, love. Amen.[130]

September 13, 2017

Holy God, bless J. K. Rowling. It is not a small thing that a generation of children have been raised on a narrative that names the seductive evils of bigotry, prejudice, and fascism. Rowling has helped shape the landscape of their moral imagination, and has populated it with characters that can be

---

128. To learn more, see http://salaamnetwork.org.

129. Horowitz, "Pope criticizes climate change deniers and Trump on DACA." With four major Atlantic hurricanes in less than three weeks, many, including Pope Francis, have been outspoken about climate change. In a speech given on September 10, 2017, Pope Francis condemned climate change skeptics saying, "history will judge world leaders who do not act against climate change."

130. McFadden, "Edith Windsor, whose same-sex marriage fight let to landmark ruling, dies at 88." Edith Windsor was a true hero to many in the LGBTQ community. The gay-rights activist's landmark case led the American Supreme Court to dismantle 1996's controversial Defense of Marriage Act (DOMA). This ensured that same-sex couples across the United States had the right to marry as well as federal benefit rights that only heterosexual married couples had prior to this 2013 case.

recognized in the real world. She has also inspired them to be like Harry Potter and, perhaps more importantly, Hermione Granger, Neville Longbottom, Ron Weasley, Luna Lovegood, and Colin Creevey. She has taught my children—and me—that sometimes it is right to fight what appears to be a losing battle, and that slowing down evil might be enough if we all take our turn.

In these Dementor-ridden days, as we pass each other bits of chocolate to get by, I give thanks for the young people who have Dumbledore's Army coins in their pockets, and I pray for the author who put them there. Amen.

September 14, 2017

God of Grace, I give thanks for those compassionate people who offer comfort, support, and care for others even while undergoing their own difficult times. May their generosity of spirit be contagious. Amen.

September 15, 2017

God of Lament, I am thinking tonight of activists and community leaders in the United States who are exhausted. Weary and worn out from the ceaseless barrage of discrimination, denigration, and death that rains down on black and brown communities. Many are protesting tonight in St. Louis, after the person who killed Anthony Lamar Smith walked free. Others are continuing the daily work of fighting white supremacy in cities and towns across the country.

Their work is a stubborn embodiment of hope that the United States can be better. It is an adamant refusal to believe the lies of racism. It is a prophetic reminder of your call for humanity to live in relationships of love and justice.

Bless them, God. Be faithful to them. Give them rest and restoration. And help the rest of us heed their call. Amen.[131]

---

131. O'Neil and Smith. "Former St. Louis officer, Jason Stockley, acquitted in shooting of black driver."

Prayers

September 16, 2017

God of Refuge, bless the California Senate, which passed a bill to limit state and local law enforcement's cooperation with federal immigration agents. Local police won't be forced into serving as agents of deportation, and people in immigrant communities won't have to be quite as fearful to report a crime or call for help. May this legislation be a model for other states, and may these lawmakers continue to show moral courage. Amen.[132]

September 17, 2017

Holy God, I pray for U2, who cancelled a concert in St. Louis after the person who killed Anthony Lamar Smith was not convicted. May all of us make it clear that racism is bad for the economy. Amen.[133]

September 18, 2017

Holy God, I ask your blessing on students who are willing to let their worldviews be dismantled in order to gain a more accurate understanding. I am awed by their bravery.

As they suffer the pain of loss and the discomfort of confusion, comfort them with your presence. Guide them toward truth, critical thinking, and self-awareness. As they listen carefully to the experiences of others, accompany them on the journey to humility. Reward them with knowledge and wisdom. Amen.

---

132. Phillips, "In message of defiance to Trump, lawmakers vote to make California a sanctuary state." California approved a "sanctuary state" bill on Saturday, September 16, 2017, that limits how local and state police interact with federal immigration agents. Forcing police officers to serve the interests of federal immigration efforts limits their ability to serve areas with a high immigrant population. It erodes trust and makes people less likely to call on the police in times of need, for fear police involvement could result in deportation of a member of the community.

133. Johnson, "U2, Ed Sheeran cancel St. Louis concerts; other events also called off." Amid numerous protests in St. Louis over Anthony Lamar Smith's death, U2 and Ed Sheeran both cancelled their shows scheduled for Sunday, September 17, 2017. Shortly after the announcement was made, Bono tweeted: "deeply saddened at what has happened in St. Louis and having to cancel our show tonight. . . I found myself reading Dr. King's speech from the National Cathedral and asking myself is this 1968 or 2017?"

Disciplined Hope

September 19, 2017

Enduring God, bless the bipartisan group of ten governors who wrote a letter opposing the Graham-Cassidy bill, which is the latest effort to get rid of the Affordable Care Act.

Gardeners have to weed all summer long. Bless the legislators who continue to pluck out each new anti-ACA bill that sprouts up. Bless the organizations, activists, and citizens that keep watching and weeding.

May we be vigilant in our care for the common good and our protection of the most vulnerable. Amen.[134]

September 20, 2017

Merciful God, I pray for every person who volunteered, donated, or prayed for those affected by Harvey and Irma, and those already working to help others in the midst of Maria. These actions state that other people—even strangers from another place—are inherently worthy of respect, dignity, and care.

I doubt that many of the volunteers and contributors and prayer warriors see their actions as political. Yet they send a message that contrasts starkly with the current administration's violent rhetoric that casually threatens millions of human lives.

Grant stamina to our compassion as the storms continue and the waters rise. Amen.

September 21, 2017

God of Courage, bless the Cahokia Quarterback's Club eight-and-under squad, who knelt during the national anthem before a game this week to support those protesting in St. Louis. Continue the work you have begun in these children. Pour your blessings on the parents, grandparents, neighbors, and aunties who are teaching them. Encourage Coach Orlando Gooden, who answered the children's questions with honesty and honored

---

134. Sullivan, Eilperin, and Snell, "New health-care plan stumbles under opposition from governors." The governors of ten states signed a letter to Senate Majority Leader Mitch McConnell and Senate Minority Leader Chuck Schumer urging against the consideration of the bill being championed by senators Lindsey Graham and Bill Cassidy. This version of the healthcare bill repeals many individual and employer mandates of the Affordable Care Act and replaces subsidies with grants.

their decision to kneel. Strengthen the community and solidarity among these young people, that they may accompany each other into positions of leadership and influence. Amen.[135]

September 22, 2017

Steadfast God, bless Senator Kamala Harris, who is calling this latest anti-healthcare bill out for the nonsense it is. Amen.[136]

September 23, 2017

God of Justice, bless Stephen Curry, LeBron James, and other athletes who refuse to accept bigotry, prejudice, and plain old stupid.

The strategy of dividing Americans against each other in order to gain power has been used for centuries. These guys are naming it.

May all people of good will in the U.S. learn something of teamwork and truth-telling from these athletes. Amen.[137]

September 24, 2017

Gracious God, I pray that there are really smart people in Washington DC who are experts on North Korean culture, history, and politics and are working diligently to avoid war. I pray they have counterparts in North Korea, South Korea, and China—smart people who are experts on the culture, history, and politics of other countries, working diligently to avoid war. I

---

135. Eschman, "Eight-year-old Cahokia football players take a knee for national anthem."

136. Decker, "At naturalization ceremony and healthcare rally, Kamala Harris goes after Trump and his GOP allies." California Senator Kamala Harris spoke at a naturalization ceremony for forty children aboard the battleship Iowa in the Port of Los Angeles on September 22, 2017. She spoke out against Donald Trump's characterization of immigrants as well as the GOP's latest healthcare plan. Sen. Harris described the team of Republicans who came up with the plan—all white men—as "this group that looks exactly like each other and not like most of us here."

137. Bonesteel and Payne, "LeBron James sticks up for Stephen Curry, calls President Trump a 'bum.'" After Stephen Curry stated that the Golden State Warriors could send a message to the White House by declining their invitation following the NBA championship, Donald Trump rescinded the invitation to the entire team. LeBron James was quick to defend Curry by calling Donald Trump a "bum" on Twitter.

pray there are policy wonks and diplomats and international peacemakers working every angle towards peace.

I do not honestly know if such people have any access to power. I worry that we are down to reality television and international conglomerates making billions off weapons and fear. But I pray, God, that there are intelligent and knowledgeable people who have a little leverage in the halls of power. And I pray you bless them. Amen.

September 25, 2017

God, I pray for senators Susan Collins, Rand Paul, and John McCain. So far, they are refusing to vote for a thrown-together mess of a bill that would cause incredible harm to millions of people.

Yep. The bar is that low. Amen.[138]

September 26, 2017

Gracious God, I pray tonight for everyone doing the difficult work of staying engaged in political discourse and attempting to remain sane.

Chaos is part of the current administration's agenda. Attacks on the common good from different directions, at different levels of government, with different vulnerable groups targeted.

If we each respond to every threat, we will be incapacitated. If we all turn away and pretend it isn't happening, we will have abdicated our responsibility to our fellows.

Teach us, oh God, to run and to rest. Grant us restorative sleep, nourishing food, sustaining beauty, and accepting friends. Give us moments of laughter and joy. Amen.

September 27, 2017

Holy God, I pray blessing on Doug Jones, a former U.S. attorney who is a candidate to represent Alabama in the Senate. Jones is a proponent of fairness, education, affordable health care, and abiding by the Constitution. He

---

138. Kaplan and Pear, "Health bill appears dead as pivotal GOP Senator declares opposition." The GOP's last-ditch effort to repeal and replace the Affordable Care Act received the final opposition on Monday, September 25, 2017, when Republican Susan Collins, John McCain, and Rand Paul all voted "no."

Prayers

speaks out against racism. His opponent, Roy Moore, openly endorses racist, heterosexist, and bigoted views; he was twice removed from the role of Chief Justice of the Alabama Supreme Court for refusing to uphold the law.

Jones is tangibly resisting the normalization of white supremacy in U.S. political discourse. He is also resisting palpable threats to the LGBTQ community. Remove every obstacle in his path, God, and allow his success to be a powerful rebuke of hatred. Amen.[139]

September 28, 2017

Steadfast God, I lift up those who marched today in St. Paul, Minnesota, to protest the proposed Enbridge Line 3 pipeline. While the Enbridge Energy company calls this a "replacement" for an older line, it would cut a new corridor of 160 miles, go over twenty watersheds, and threaten both water supplies and wild rice fields. A coalition of twenty-eight groups—from Black Lives Matter to the Sierra Club to the Leech Lake Band of Ojibwe—participated, with hundreds of people marching together.

Pour out your Spirit among us, God, that we all may recognize our interdependence, shared vulnerability, mutual concerns, and collaborative power. Amen.[140]

September 29, 2017

God of Compassion, bless the companies who are trying to help Puerto Rico. The current administration was slow off the mark to respond to Hurricane Maria, has yet to provide adequate resources, and is hesitant to commit to long-term efforts. While a better federal response is still desperately needed, some companies are stepping up. The University of Central Florida will offer in-state tuition rates to students displaced by Maria; AT&T is trying to help connect family members with special services; JetBlue is unrolling 35 different initiatives and already doing relief flights; both Carnival and Royal Caribbean cruise lines are using their ships for relief efforts; Tesla is sending battery packs; Yale New Haven Health System is sending 30,000 pounds of medical supplies, which United

---

139. Weigel, "Who is Doug Jones, and can he defeat Roy Moore in conservative Alabama?"

140. Kraker, "At Line 3 Pipeline hearing, it's environment vs. jobs."

Disciplined Hope

Airlines is transporting for free; and I'm sure there are more examples. I pray blessing on the people of good will in each of these companies. Amen.[141]

September 30, 2017

God of Strength, bless Carmen Yulin Cruz Soto, mayor of San Juan. She has been working tirelessly for the people of her city. She told the truth about the horrific conditions after Maria, rejecting the administration's falsehood that what is happening in Puerto Rico is "a good-news story." With every fiber of her being, this woman is resisting the colonialist, racist greed of the current occupant of the White House.

God, I ask that you bless Mayor Cruz with aid to her community, with the necessities of life, and with a way forward for Puerto Rico. I ask that you pour out your Spirit upon her, affording her words and actions unforeseen power to change the relationship between Puerto Rico and the United States for the better, to reveal the racism of this administration to those who have not yet perceived it, and to spark an overwhelming tide of concern and concrete help from their fellow U.S. Citizens. Bless her truth-telling commitment to her community with transformative might. Amen.[142]

October 1, 2017

Gracious God, I pray for pastors, rabbis, priests, imams, and other clergy who serve their communities with tender care. Daily they show forth mercy and witness to the constant presence of divine love. Amen.

---

141. Korosec, "Tesla is helping Puerto Rico get power after Hurricane Maria." Sloan, "Cruise lines extend aid to hard-hit Caribbean islands." Christensen, "AT&T helps you locate loved ones in Puerto Rico after Hurricane Maria." Figueroa, "Mainland colleges offer in-state tuition to students affected by Hurricane Maria." Pierce, "Medical supplies heading to Puerto Rico 'con amor.'" Hallinan, "JetBlue launches hurricane relief plan for Puerto Rico."

142. Hernandez, Schmidt, Selk and Wan, "Trump called San Juan's mayor a weak leader. Here's what her leadership looks like." Carmen Yulin Cruz Soto, the mayor of Puerto Rico's capital San Juan, appeared on national television shortly after hurricane Maria devastated the island. She asked Donald Trump to act quickly on hurricane relief and called the situation a "humanitarian crisis." Donald Trump responded on Twitter, criticizing Yulin Cruz for her "poor leadership ability" and saying that Puerto Rico "wants everything to be done for them."

Prayers

October 2, 2017

Holy God, bless every person advocating for reasonable gun control. Amen.

October 3, 2017

Holy God, bless Supreme Court Justice Ruth Bader Ginsburg. Continue to guide her fierce sense of fairness and acute intelligence. Renew, strengthen, and expand her influence and power. Allow this coming season to be shaped by her wisdom. Amen.

October 4, 2017

Eternal God, I lift up the BLM protesters in St. Louis who continue to resist state-sanctioned violence against black and brown bodies. Bless them with your palpable presence, with strength, with comfort, and with healing.

And God, bless the rest of us with better memories. Every day brings a new story into the center of public life. Some are vital, some are trivial. Either way they quickly fade from view as the cameras focus on the next story. Protect us from the "attention economy" that trades our concentration for cash. Guard us from our own eagerness for distraction. Remind us that the central story of existence is of love, holy and human, and help us take our places in that eternal tale. Amen.

October 5, 2017

Holy God, bless every person attempting to save the Iran nuclear deal, if only to prevent the absolute loss of credibility for the United States in any future international negotiations. Amen.[143]

---

143. Landler and Sanger, "Trump to force congress to act on Iran nuclear deal." Donald Trump decertified the landmark international deal to curb Iran's nuclear program; a step that potentially could cause the 2015 accord to completely unravel. The Trump administration is expected to roll out a broader U.S. strategy on Iran that would be more confrontational.

Disciplined Hope

October 6, 2017

God of Strength, bless Cecile Richards, president of Planned Parenthood, and everyone else who helps give women and families access to safe contraception. May all of us who respect women's agency and well-being join Richards in actively resisting the regressive policies of the current administration. Amen.[144]

October 8, 2017

God of Wisdom, bless the Tow Center for Digital Journalism at Columbia University. Among other things, they are investigating the reach of Russian-controlled accounts on Facebook during the election. Give them evidence and insight in efforts to protect democracy. Amen.[145]

October 9, 2017

God of Abundance, bless everyone who feeds people. To offer food to one another is a fundamental and powerful way to affirm life, not death, and to foster community, not isolation. So tonight I am praying for every person who brings snacks or cooks dinner, makes kimchi or cans tomatoes, donates to a food bank or does all they can to get a meal for the kids. Everyone who is baking more than usual this season, taking potato salad to the potluck, or sharing French fries during lunch. Nourish in us this impulse towards life and wholeness. Amen.

---

144. Goodstein, Pear, and Ruiz, "Trump administration rolls back birth control mandate." On Friday, October 6, 2017, the Trump administration announced that they planned to eliminate the Affordable Care Act's requirement that all insurance plans must cover birth control without co-pay. Cecile Richards, president of Planned Parenthood, condemned the decision by stating that "birth control is not controversial—it's healthcare the vast majority of women will use in the course of their lifetime."

145. Timberg, "Russian propaganda may have been shared hundreds of millions of times, new research says." Jonathan Albright, research director at Columbia University's Tow Center for Digital Journalism, revealed that a number of Facebook pages were being controlled by Russians and carrying out propaganda campaigns for the Kremlin during the election. "They are feeding into the outrage—and it's easy to do, because outrage and emotion is how people share" Albright revealed.

Prayers

October 10, 2017

God of Tenacity, I pray blessing on all those who advocate for practices and policies to address climate change. Keep them going through this time of setbacks. Inspire them with new strategies and creative approaches. Sustain them with support from unexpected places. Amen.

October 11, 2017

God of Truth, I lift in prayer, praise, and blessing those brave souls who have "come out" as LGBTQ in communities where welcome was not assured. They have taught me that you are bigger than I imagined, that we are more wonderfully varied than I knew, that joy is a form of reverence, that grace includes an imperative to grow, and that love really can change the world. Amen.

October 12, 2017

God of Hope, I give thanks for the heart-rendering brilliance of Actors Theatre's production of Tony Kushner's *Angels in America*. Bless the members of this particular company, and bless the larger theatrical community. Their creativity and craft resists dehumanizing forces through truth-telling, imagination, communal meaning-making, artistry, and beauty. Amen.[146]

October 14, 2017

Holy God, tonight I lift up Habitat for Humanity, which has been building and repairing homes for forty years. Habitat has announced a long-term plan and commitment to Puerto Rico.

For those who are steadfast, I pray. Amen.[147]

---

146. Kramer, "Actors 'Angels in America' takes flight—review."
147. "Habitat for Humanity prepares long-term recovery plan for Puerto Rico."

Disciplined Hope

October 15, 2017

God of Hope, bless the Howard University cheerleaders, who have been kneeling during the national anthem for a year to protest police brutality. And bless the soccer team from Berlin that knelt in solidarity.

Multiply our efforts at communion, God, and add to our attempts to foster the common good. Help us to see the power of good will with and for each other. Amen.[148]

October 16, 2017

Sustaining God, bless the attorneys general from 18 states, as well as Washington DC, who are suing the current administration to stop the Occupant's sabotage of the Affordable Care Act. May they be vigilant in protecting democracy and upholding the rule of law. Amen.[149]

October 17, 2017

God of Justice, bless U.S. District Judge Derrick K. Watson, who blocked the implementation of the current administration's third attempt at a Muslim ban. Amen.[150]

October 18, 2017

God of Miracles, I give thanks for the people of World Kitchen Central, including chefs Jose Andres and Jose Enrique, who have served one million

---

148. Tracy, "Howard cheerleaders add voices to the anthem debate by taking a knee." The Howard University cheer squad began kneeling in protest in September 2016. Howard University is only 2 miles away from the White House and is one of 107 historically black colleges and universities in the country.

149. Abutaleb and Levine, "Eighteen states sue to block Trum's cut to Obamacare subsidies."

150. Yee, "Judge temporarily halts new version of Trump's travel ban." For the third time in a year, Derrick K. Watson, a federal judge in Hawaii issued a temporary injunction against the latest travel ban revised by Donald Trump. Judge Watson blocked the current travel ban because it "lacks sufficient findings that the entry of more than 150 million nationals from six specified countries would be detrimental to the interests of the United States."

Prayers

meals to those affected by Hurricane Maria in Puerto Rico. May their incredible work be an example to us all. Amen.[151]

October 20, 2017

God of Joy, bless Laura Ellis, a music professor at the University of Florida. When a white supremacist gave a talk on campus, Ellis played "Lift Every Voice and Sing" on the carillon (the bell tower that can be heard all over campus). I imagine the many people who had gathered to stand against white supremacy enjoyed this rendition of the black national anthem. I bet they sang along.

For those who resist with joy and style, we give thanks. Amen.[152]

October 21, 2017

God of Truth, bless the Weather Channel, which has been working to remind the rest of America about the ongoing crisis in Puerto Rico. May their work spur the rest of us to advocate for immediate relief and long-term policies to rebuild Puerto Rico. Amen.[153]

October 22, 2017

Holy God, I pray for Senator Sherrod Brown, who stated clearly that white supremacists are influencing the current administration.

May we all tell the truth and shame the devil. Amen.[154]

---

151. Carman, "After Maria, Jose Andres and his team have prepared more hot meals in Puerto Rico than the Red Cross." After three weeks in Puerto Rico, Jose Andres, a Washington DC-based chef just served his one-millionth meal. Arriving in Puerto Rico shortly after Hurricane Maria devastated the island, Andres set up fifteen kitchens around the island and partnered with ten food trucks to help feed the citizens of Puerto Rico.

152. Modisett, "Carillon plays 'Lift Every Voice and Sing' as Richard Spencer peaks in Florida."

153. Abbruzzese, "The Weather Channel wants you to know there's a more pressing issue than the weather right now." One month after Hurricane Maria hit Puerto Rico, when many people in the U.S. mainland had turned our minds to other things, the Weather Channel website and mobile app ran the headline, "AMERICA, THIS IS STILL HAPPENING." The front-page stories were all focused on the ongoing crisis in Puerto Rico.

154. Link, "Sen. Sherrod Brown: Steve Bannon is a 'white supremacist.'" In an

Disciplined Hope

October 23, 2017

Fierce God of Joy, I pray for Harry Belafonte. At 90 years old, he recently made a public appearance in which he recounted his life in music and activism, warned the U.S. that the current administration is extremely dangerous, and offered his continuing conviction that we shall overcome.

Thank you, God, for such strong and gifted leaders in the work of justice. Help us continue the struggle. Amen.[155]

October 24, 2017

Holy God, bless Senators Jeff Flake and Bob Corker for telling the truth and having some, even minimal, standards. I don't agree with them on many issues, and I wish they both would have made strong statements this time last year, but I am still grateful for their refusal to acquiesce indefinitely to the dangerous and deceitful behavior of the Occupant. I don't know if their actions are the best possible strategies. I suspect we might need a plethora of tactics and approaches. And in these days when every fear is being fed and watered daily, I respect every speck of courage.

For every other Republican representative, the cover of the collective has been blown. Amen.[156]

October 25, 2017

God of Liberation, I pray tonight for every person working to end mass incarceration. The concept of for-profit prisons—creating financial incentives

---

interview on Sunday, October 22, 2017, on CNN's State of the Union, Senator Sherrod Brown said, "Steve Bannon is a white supremacist and Stephen Miller seems to be." These comments came in in response to representative Frederica Wilson's interview with *The New York Times* the previous week stating, "the White House itself is full of white supremacists."

155. Elk, "Harry Belafonte tells crowd at likely last public appearance: 'We Shall Overcome.'" Entertainer and civil rights activist Harry Belafonte used his final public appearance to issue a warning about the future of the nation. According to Belafonte, "America made a mistake" when it elected Donald Trump as president.

156. Rucker, "Trump punches back at Flake and Corker, claims a 'love fest' of support in Senate." Republican Senators Jeff Flake and Bob Corker criticized Trump's $1.5 trillion tax cut, stating that Donald Trump is dangerous and could put the United States on the path to World War III. Trump responded on Twitter that the rest of the Republican senators (Flake and Corker aside) had a "love fest" for him complete with standing ovations.

Prayers

to put people in captivity—draws deep from the worst aspects of U.S. history. It is antithetical to the gospel of Jesus Christ and to the ethics of compassion shared by many religious and humanitarian traditions.

In this moment when U.S. policies are moving backward on these issues, bless those who combat this evil system. Sustain and encourage them. Grant the rest of us moral clarity, systemic analysis, and the will to resist. Amen.

October 26, 2017

God of Hope, this evening I got to spend time with white, straight, male mainline Christians who have been fighting racism with their theology, energy, and checkbooks for many years.

Bless them for their witness. Help us remember that all are welcome to work for the common good. Amen.

October 27, 2017

Holy God, bless the seven members of the Fairfax County, Virginia, school board who voted to change the name of J. E. B. Stuart High School to Justice High. Amen.[157]

October 28, 2017

God of Love, I pray blessing tonight on all the people of good will who stood against white nationalism and racist hatred in Tennessee today. The neo-Nazis had planned a second rally tomorrow, but canceled it in the face of today's resistance.

May those who stood for love today rest well tonight. May their friends and neighbors be moved to emulate their courage. Amen.[158]

---

157. Truong, "Fairfax County school district votes to rename J. E. B. Stuart High." After much deliberation, the Fairfax County School Board voted to change the name of J. E. B. Stuart High School—named after a Confederate soldier—to Justice High, in honor of all those who have worked for equality and justice.

158. Jenkins, "White Nationalists hold 'White Lives Matter' rallies in Tennessee." A 'White Lives Matter' rally was held in Shelbyville, Tennessee, on October 28, 2017. Some 200 white nationalists showed up and were met by twice as many counter protestors. Counter protestors played Martin Luther King Jr.'s *I Have a Dream* speech over their own

Disciplined Hope

October 29, 2017

God of Love, bless federal judge Colleen Kollar-Kotelly, who blocked implementation of the Occupant's ban of people who are transgender serving in the military. And bless the brave plaintiffs in the case, five transgender women currently serving. Amen.[159]

October 31, 2017

God of Mischief, bless every parent, auntie, grandparent, or friend who helped these kids get dressed up just to have fun. Thank you for every bit of silliness and sweetness this day. Amen.

November 1, 2017

God of Love, I give thanks for all the saints who have gone before us. We are not alone, but surrounded by a great cloud of witnesses. Relationships of love are not severed by death, but held securely in the hands of God. Amen.[160]

November 2, 2017

Holy God, I'm still praying for Robert Mueller and his team. May they find the truth. And may the people of the United States value truth, facts, and evidence. Amen.

November 3, 2017

Holy God, I pray this evening for those who are speaking out about sexual harassment and assault. And I pray for those who have spoken out before.

---

speakers, drowning out the National Socialist speakers. In Murfreesboro, thirty white nationalists showed up for a separate rally on the same day and were met by over 500 counter protestors.

159. Philipps, "Judge blocks Trump's ban on transgender troops in military."
160. November 1 is All Saints Day in many Christian traditions.

Prayers

(A special blessing on Anita Hill, please God.) May the collective courage of truth-tellers spark lasting change for the better. Amen.[161]

November 4, 2017

God of Life, I give thanks for the protesters in Hawaii who met the Occupant with pithy signs. My favorite: "Welcome to Kenya."

Bless us with humor in the midst of struggle. Amen.[162]

November 5, 2017

God of Life, I pray for every person who curses vehemently when told, "now is not the time to talk about gun control" or "don't politicize this." May they swear with the tongues of angels. May their bold impatience with stupidity inspire others to intervene in the NRA-sponsored, money-driven, death-dealing, immoral bat-shittery of American gun laws. Amen.[163]

November 6, 2017

Gracious God, tonight I lift up all who have worked with the Princeton and Slavery Project, including Professor Martha Sandweiss, Craig Hollander, and Joseph Yannielli. Telling the truth about our past is necessary to create a better future. Amen.[164]

---

161. Blair, "Women are speaking up about harassment and abuse."

162. Parker and Teague, "Trump proves an eager tourist in Hawaii." President Barack Obama was born in Hawaii. Donald Trump repeatedly spread lies about Obama's place of birth, saying he was born in Kenya.

163. Montgomery et al., "Gunman kills at least 26 in attack." On November 5, a man killed twenty-six people at First Baptist Church in Sutherland Springs, TX, during Sunday morning worship. He was armed with a military-style rifle.

164. Spensley and Ting, "U. launches Princeton and Slavery website." The history of Princeton University, like that of many academic institutions in the United States, is intertwined with the history of slavery. For example, a sale of enslaved persons took place on campus in 1766. Princeton is exemplary in doing the work of researching and acknowledging this history. See https://slavery.princeton.edu/.

Disciplined Hope

November 7, 2017

Holy God, I lift up every person who voted in today's elections. Bless us with democracy. Nurture our hope for equality and good governance. Inspire us to work together for the common good. Amen.

November 11, 2017

Merciful God, today I give thanks for those who make the effort to encourage the people around them. We are surrounded by messages telling us to fear one another and compete with one another. Then along come these gracious souls who call out strengths, not weaknesses; who remember accidental kindness, not accidental foolishness. These silly people act as if the world is not ruled by scarcity in a zero-sum game. They act like there is plenty of room and love for all of us.

I ask you to bless them, God, but it is clear that you already have, for they know something of divine abundance. Bless the rest of us, that we might know it, too. Amen.

November 12, 2017

God of Justice, bless the American Bar Association for telling the truth about some of the Occupant's judicial nominees—that they are "not qualified." Bless them with back-up, God. May they not stand alone in resisting this damage to our federal courts. Amen.[165]

November 13, 2017

God of Wisdom, this year has certainly expanded my prayer list. People and businesses and groups I did not expect to be politically engaged have pressed toward the common good in multiple ways. Tonight I pray for the people of GQ magazine, who honored Colin Kaepernick as citizen of the

---

165. Williams, "Senate oks two lawyers ABA says 'not qualified.'" On November 9, the Senate Judiciary Committed approved two lawyers for judicial appointments despite the fact that the American Bar Association—"which has been vetting judicial candidates since the 1950s"—declared them unqualified and gave them the lowest possible ranking.

year. Bless them. May there be more and more resistance from unexpected quarters. Amen.[166]

November 14, 2017

God of Grace, I pray tonight for Alabama Republicans who have decided not to vote for Roy Moore.

May none of us be so partisan as to overlook evil because it plays on our team.

Grant us discernment, that we might be self-reflective and self-critical instead of assuming those with whom we identify are always right.

At the same time, grant us moral courage, that we might avoid the laziness of false-equivalencies, what-about-ism, and cynical abandonment of ethical standards.

Help all of us be willing to learn, grow, and change as we seek a better future. Amen.[167]

November 15, 2017

Steadfast God, I pray for the Democrats in Congress who are resisting the proposed tax bill that primarily benefits the wealthy. The bill now includes deconstruction of the Affordable Care Act. Republicans tried to pass a "healthcare" bill that was really a tax cut. That didn't work. Now they are trying to pass a "tax cut" that is also an attack on healthcare. God bless the elected officials who remain vigilant in the face of numerous, drawn-out, multi-faceted threats to the social well-being of the United States. Give them stamina. Give us perseverance. Amen.[168]

November 16, 2017

God of Hope, I lift up the Black Student Union at DuPont Manual High School in Louisville, Kentucky. The group organized a sit-in this week to protest principal Jerry Mayes's discriminatory comments to African American students and to a transgender student. I give thanks for the 100+

---

166. The Editors of GQ, "Colin Kaepernick is GQ's 2017 Citizen of the Year."
167. Sullivan et al., "National Republican move against Roy Moore grows."
168. Rappeport and Kaplan, "Tax bill thrown into uncertainty."

students who demonstrated. Grant them tenacity in their work for justice, that they may influence our country's future. Amen.[169]

November 21, 2017

God of Jesus Christ, I lift up the organizers, authors, and signers of the Boston Declaration. May all Christians who believe that following Jesus means working for justice speak clearly this day. Amen.[170]

November 22, 2017

Holy God, bless the proprietors of Rocklands Farm in Maryland. An event was booked at their venue through a third party. When the event turned out to be a gathering of white nationalists, the people of Rocklands Farm asked them to leave and returned their money.

May we all be so clear in our values. Amen.[171]

November 23, 2017

Steadfast God, bless those who are working to protect net neutrality. Amen.[172]

November 24, 2017

Triune God, I lift up tonight everyone who sees the importance of community, the reality of interdependence, and the harm that can be done by illusions of rugged individualism. Amen.

---

169. Hansen and Dawson, "Black Student Union holds sit-in."

170. The Boston Declaration is a statement signed by hundreds of Christian leaders calling for a rejection of racism, anti-Semitism, Islamophobia, xenophobia, sexism, and heterosexism. While there are evangelical leaders supporting the rhetoric, policies, and personal conduct of the current administration, there are also many Christians who find these contradictory to the gospel of Jesus Christ. For the full statement, see: https://thebostondeclaration.com/blog/2017/11/18/the-boston-declaration.

171. Stein, "Richard Spencer hosted an event."

172. Newcomb, "The backlash is building over the plan to gut net neutrality." For an example of net neutrality concerns, see: Hsu, "F.C.C. plan to roll back net neutrality."

Prayers

November 25, 2017

God of Justice, I pray for those who work to secure and protect voting rights. Grant them victory over every attempt at suppression. Amen.[173]

November 26, 2017

Holy God, tonight I pray for those who daily slog through the profoundly unsexy work of being responsible citizens. Those who read and listen, weigh arguments and evidence, vote and volunteer. If the United States finds its footing again, it will be due to their efforts, to the quiet heroism of the Hufflepuffs of American politics.

Between threats to net neutrality, a tax scheme that benefits the wealthy, and the intentional destruction of the State Department, I am not feeling optimistic tonight. But I recognize the embodied hope of the daily sloggers—who relentlessly call their elected officials and contribute to the ACLU and participate in local elections—and I see that hope is holy. Even if this ship goes down, I want to be in their company. Even when I am not optimistic, I will call and contribute and participate just to be faithful to the holy hope I see in them.

Bless them. Amen.

November 27, 2017

Holy God, bless Senator Elizabeth Warren for fighting the current administration's reverse-Robin Hood policies and proposals that take money from the poor and give money to the rich. She is clearly driving the Occupant even further round the bend.

I also pray tonight for the Navajo veterans who exemplified both honor and truth-telling in response to the Occupant's racism.

May we all be honorable, honest, infuriating obstacles to hate and greed in the White House. Amen.[174]

---

173. Wines, "Culling voter rolls." There have been ongoing battles in several states over gerrymandering, voter ID laws, and culling voter rolls. Some cities have limited opportunities to vote by cutting back on hours when polling places are open, lowering the number of polling places, and locating them in areas most friendly to the party in power. Activists around the country are working to stop these efforts at voter suppression.

174. Davis, "Trump mocks Warren." On November 27, at a White House ceremony honoring Navajo veterans of World War II, Trump repeated his use of the term

Disciplined Hope

November 28, 2017

Well, God, another day of crazy here. The "tax reform" plan moving forward would help the rich and hurt the poor, the demise of net neutrality would further hinder democracy, nuclear war looks alarmingly plausible (but at least they fired the expert diplomats!), membership in white-supremacist groups is on the rise, and climate change is an unfolding disaster. And you know I have barely scratched the surface with this U.S.-centered list.

We could do with a little help around here.

It is not easy to keep struggling when the odds look so damn long.

Tonight I'm praying for the Appalachians who showed up in Charleston, West Virginia today to try and save the Clean Power Plan, an Obama-era policy that hasn't yet been enacted. Under the current administration, the EPA opposes the plan to decrease carbon emissions.

A mix of health advocates, environmentalists, and those who have been harmed by the fossil fuel industry attended the public hearing to tell the truth and work for justice even when it seems futile.

In particular, I pray for Stanley Sturgill, a retired coal miner with black lung. I honor his courage for resisting a powerful industry that trades human health and ecological wellbeing for profit, and for doing it in the heart of coal country.

Grant the rest of us a measure of such courage and perseverance. Amen.[175]

November 29, 2017

Holy God, I pray for every Muslim person who read, heard, or watched the news and somehow managed to get through the day continuing to practice a loving faith in the face of hatred. Amen.[176]

"Pocahontas" for Senator Elizabeth Warren. The president of the Navajo Nation, Russell Begaye, "called the president's mention of Pocahontas 'derogatory' and 'disrespectful to Indian nations.'"

175. Sturgill said, "Our health, environment and global climate are actively being destroyed. And it is clear to me that EPA Administrator Scott Pruitt and President Trump are accelerating and cheering on the damage . . . I have come here today to ask you to stop. For the sake of my grandchildren and yours, I call on you to strengthen, not repeal, the Clean Power Plan." Dennis, "In the heart of coal country."

176. Baker and Sullivan, "Trump shares inflammatory anti-Muslim videos, and Britain's leader condemns them." On November 29, Trump shared three videos from Britain First, "a fringe British ultranationalist group," showing acts of violence and claiming they

Prayers

November 30, 2017

God of Solidarity, I give thanks tonight for the lay readers (neither academics nor clergy) from Kentucky who selected James Cone's *The Cross and the Lynching Tree* to receive the 2018 Grawemeyer Award in Religion. Amen.[177]

December 1, 2017

God of Mercy, I pray tonight for the many faith organizations that have been resisting the Senate tax proposal. In a joint letter, Buddhist, Jewish, Muslim, Christian, and Sikh faith leaders renounced the proposed legislation as unjust and immoral.

Renew our energy, restore our strength, and strengthen our bonds of solidarity as we continue to work together for the common good. Amen.[178]

December 2, 2017

Steadfast God, I pray for Matthew Dunlap, Maine's Secretary of State and a member of the Presidential Advisory Commission on Election Integrity. Wary that this commission was put in place to add an appearance of credibility to the Occupant's false claims that millions of illegal votes were cast, Dunlap accepted the position out of commitment to the election process. However, the work of the committee is being done by only certain

---

were perpetrated by Muslims. One of the videos actually showed two Dutch boys. The others were four years old and were recorded in Syria and Egypt during times of political turmoil. British Prime Minister Theresa May rebuked Trump, saying "It is wrong for the president to have done this."

177. Gillespie, "Grawemeyer winner on links between." The Grawemeyer Award in Religion honors works that express potentially world-changing ideas with such clarity that they are accessible to people beyond the academy. The selection process for this award includes vetting by experts, but the final choice relies on readers who are not professional academics. These readers chose Cone's book, which analyzes the role of Christianity in the racism of the United States and the lynching of thousands of black and brown men, women, and children. These lay readers were surprised to learn, after selecting Cone's book, that he is one of the most famous and influential theologians of the last hundred years.

178. Anapol, "Faith leaders write to Senate." Over 2,400 representatives from a variety of religious traditions wrote a joint letter to Senate Majority Leader Mitch McConnell and Senate Minority Leader Charles Schumer asking them to oppose the Tax Cuts and Jobs Act. They stated that the plan "violates our moral principles of equality, justice and fairness."

members, while others are kept in the dark. Dunlap is suing the commission for information.

It is hard to resist something attacking from so many angles at once. I am grateful that Dunlap is focused on the integrity of the election process in 2018. His suit might bring to light plans of further voter suppression.

Help us, God, to use the resources of resistance well—with division of labor, varieties of specialized concern, and the capacity to come together across all fronts to address immediate needs. Grant us wisdom for the struggle. Amen.[179]

December 3, 2017

God of Hope, bless the multitudes who are calling representatives, rallying, and demonstrating in opposition to the unjust and immoral tax proposal. May their voices be heard and heeded. Amen.[180]

December 4, 2017

Creator God, bless the people who run Patagonia as they call attention to the Occupant's attack on protected lands. Amen.[181]

December 5, 2017

God of Courage, bless the pilots in Germany who refuse to deport people whose requests for asylum have been rejected. Yes. Yes. Yes. Amen.[182]

---

179. Dunlap, "I'm on Trump's voter fraud commission."

180. Van Dam, "Is the GOP tax plan."

181. Lee, "'The President stole your land," and Andrews, "'The President Stole Your Land.'" On December 4, Trump reduced the size of two national monuments in Utah, Bears Ears and Grand Staircase-Escalante, by nearly 2 million acres. The outdoor clothing company Patagonia changed its website to read, "The President Stole Your Land."

182. Sharman, "Pilots stop 222 asylum seekers." Germany declared Afghanistan "a safe country of origin" for some of the people seeking asylum from violence and repression there. Pilots have halted deportations by simply refusing to allow those being deported on board.

Prayers

December 6, 2017

God of Jacob, I am wrestling tonight. Are we not limping enough already?

For those who are willing to wrestle with complicated texts, complex histories, current events, and faithful commitment, I pray. Concretely, this means I am praying for every religious leader—of any tradition—who is condemning the Occupant's rash and even hateful declaration regarding Jerusalem.

Please, God: bless us. Amen.[183]

December 7, 2017

God of Solidarity, bless the hundreds of immigrant-rights activists who participated in nationwide demonstrations yesterday supporting DREAM Act legislation. More than 200 activists were arrested in DC.

I give thanks for their witness. I lift up their example. I ask for divine assistance in the ongoing struggle for justice. Amen.[184]

December 9, 2017

God of Justice, bless those involved with PICO, a community-organizing network that does the steady, thoughtful work of transformative activism. Continue to inspire and guide them. Grant them support and resources. Afford them victories. Amen.[185]

December 11, 2017

God of Wisdom, bless the members of the Monday night book club at Providence Presbyterian Church in Charlotte, NC. I give thanks for their curiosity and their commitment to faithful, prayerful social and political engagement. Amen.

---

183. Landler, "Trump recognizes Jerusalem." On December 6, Trump formally recognized Jerusalem as the capital of Israel, a political move that supports and encourages the oppression of the Palestinian people.

184. Guadalupe, "'Do the right thing.'" In September, Trump announced the end of DACA. Dreamers have been in a state of uncertainty ever since.

185. For more information, see: https://www.piconetwork.org/.

Disciplined Hope

December 12, 2017

Sweet baby Jesus, pour out blessings upon every person in Alabama who overcame lines or obstacles to cast a vote today.

I'll be here weeping in Kentucky. Amen.[186]

December 14, 2017

Righteous God, bless the editorial board of USA Today. Yesterday's article on the Occupant was an act of resistance to the normalization of sexism, racism, and deceitfulness. Amen.[187]

December 17, 2017

God of Jubilation, on this third Sunday of Advent, also called Gaudete Sunday, many Christians mark the importance of joy. To share joy with others is a reflection of heavenly communion. The Bible says that perfect love casts out fear. I suspect that perfect joy casts out division.

Tonight I pray for all who are joyful, even if it is sporadic, or only a little. I pray that you might bless us all with unexpected joys, and that we might be open and eager to share joy with our families, neighbors, friends, coworkers, the stranger on the bus, and the cashier in the grocery store.

This, too, is resistance. Amen.

December 19, 2017

Dear God, I ask your blessings on those left-of-center who are not beguiled by purity politics. Those who recognize that a great variety of strategies might be needed to change our world for the better. Those who are more committed to the common good than to their own superior knowledge, perception, or analysis. Those who greet all who struggle for justice as kin. May their solidarity bear great fruit. Amen.

---

186. Bloch, "Alabama election results." Doug Jones defeated Roy Moore in the Alabama special election to fill the U.S. Senate seat left vacant when Jeff Sessions became Attorney General. Although Roy Moore was a reprehensible candidate, it seemed quite possible that Alabama, traditionally deeply Republican, would support him.

187. The Editorial Board, "Will Trump's lows ever hit rock bottom?"

Prayers

December 20, 2017

God of Mercy, I pray tonight for the Gifford Law Center to Prevent Gun Violence. Founded by former Congresswoman Gabrielle Giffords and her astronaut husband Captain Mark Kelly, this organization is currently suing the administration for refusing to divulge evidence of the extent of coordination between the administration and the gun lobby. The Gifford Center wants to know if the gun lobby is directing the Occupant's appointment of particular judicial nominees.

I admire the clarity of thought and purpose. I pray the suit is a wild success. Amen.[188]

December 22, 2017

Holy God, I give thanks for the United Nations General Assembly, which voted overwhelmingly to demand that the United States rescind the Occupant's decision to recognize Jerusalem as the capital of Israel. I pray for global leaders who resist reckless political power plays. I pray for peace in Jerusalem, liberation in Palestine, and global solidarity among those who seek the common good. Amen.[189]

December 24, 2017

God of Hope, I pray for all who seek, protect, mind, await, and become the Light. Amen.

December 28, 2017

God of Lament, tonight I pray for Erica Garner, who worked to end police brutality after her father, Eric Garner, was choked to death by a cop in 2014. Erica Garner is in a coma and has been declared brain dead after suffering a heart attack.

---

188. For more information, see: lawcenter.giffords.org/.

189. Gladstone and Lander, "Defying Tump, U.N. General Assembly condemns." Although Trump threated to cut aid to countries who voted against his decision to recognize Jerusalem as the capital of Israel, the UN General Assembly still passed a resolution demanding that the U.S. rescind Trump's declaration. This resolution is nonbinding, but symbolically demonstrates the international community's repudiation of Trump.

Disciplined Hope

She is 27 years old. She has two children.

I pray for perfect healing for Erica Garner. I pray stable, enduring, loving care for her children. I pray comfort for the Garner family and community.

For the rest of us, I ask that we be bold enough and honest enough to lament this terrible loss as part of the sweeping harm of racism and inequality. Erica Garner was subjected to enormous stress—as are so many black women—due to structures of oppression. Grant us the courage to truly repent, first by acknowledging the brokenness of our social structures, recognizing the ways in which we benefit from them, suffer from them, ignore them, and let them continue to operate. The second aspect of repentance is a course correction. Grant us the will and bravery to change, replace, transform, dismantle, or disable the systems of oppression that shape our common life. May we honor both Erica and Eric Garner by committing ourselves to making the world more just for the next generation. Amen.[190]

December 29, 2017

God of Peace, I pray for the sixty-three Israeli teenagers who refuse to be drafted into the Israeli army. In a letter to the Prime Minister and other government officials, the teens stated they would not be part of the occupation and oppression of Palestinians. They are willing to face prosecution and jail rather than comply with such extreme injustice.

Bless them, God, and may their witness foster bravery in us all. Amen.[191]

December 30, 2017

God of Rainbows, I pray for the neighbors next door to Mike Pence's vacation home in Colorado, who put up a sign at the end of the drive reading "Make America Gay Again." Continue to bless them with humor and love. Amen.[192]

---

190. Goldstein, "Eric Gardner's 27-year-old daughter."
191. Moore, "Israeli teens refuse to serve in military."
192. Phillips, "Mike Pence's Colorado neighbors troll him."

Prayers

December 31, 2017

God of Hope, I ask blessing on those who are tending life. New moms and dads. Grown children caring for aging parents. Partners and neighbors supporting loved ones who are injured or ill.

Tending life is an act of hope and an affirmation of the surpassing value of kindness, compassion, friendship, and love. Amen.

January 1, 2018

Holy God, bless those who leave their warm homes this cold night to offer blankets and shelter to those with no respite from the weather. Help us build a society where no one is left out in the cold. Amen.

January 9, 2018

God of Justice, bless the federal judges who ruled that the highly gerrymandered North Carolina congressional district map must be redrawn. Bless the lawyers and advocacy groups who filed the lawsuit. Bless the people of North Carolina who have stubbornly refused to acquiesce to the violation of democracy. Bless us all with a sense of ownership, accountability, investment, and vigilance regarding our democratic processes. Amen.[193]

January 10, 2018

God of Grace, I lift up U.S. District Judge William Alsup, who ruled that Deferred Action for Childhood Arrivals legislation (DACA) must remain in place while legal challenges to the Occupant's decision to rescind it are resolved. May we all be wary of decisions to round people up, kick them out, or send them into dangerous situations. Amen.[194]

---

193. Blinder and Wines, "North Carolina is ordered to redraw its congressional map." Judges ruled North Carolina's election districts for U.S. Congress unconstitutional on Tuesday, January 9, 2018. The judges deemed the districts to be partisan gerrymandering and gave lawmakers until January 29 to correct the problem.

194. Hawkins, "Trump vs. Trump, again: Judge cites presidential tweets as he blocks DACA phaseout."

Disciplined Hope

January 11, 2018

God of Creation, I give thanks for the Republican-controlled Federal Energy Regulatory Commission, which rejected the current administration's plan to prop up coal-fired and nuclear power plants over other energy sources.

I suspect I disagree with every person on this committee on almost every political and environmental issue. I give thanks for them anyway for this action, and I pray blessing upon them. May the beauty of creation inspire them—and me—to ongoing action. Amen.[195]

January 12, 2018

Merciful God, I have a lot of prayers tonight. Earlier this week a man named Imamu Baraka saw a woman being left outside in thirty-degree weather, wearing a hospital gown and socks, as she was discharged from a hospital in Baltimore. Baraka videotaped the event and attempted to help the woman.

First, I pray for this woman. Please come to her aid, God; surround her with support and enable her healing in every way, including healing from this trauma.

Second, I pray for the hospital staff who discharged her in this way. They, too, need healing, from whatever instigated this betrayal of their own humanity.

Third, I pray for myself. I cannot say with certainty that I would have stopped to help this woman, or risked losing a job by refusing to discharge her. My humanity is also fragile and easily fractured.

Fourth, I pray for Baraka, that he may never be without warmth and shelter and friends.

Finally, God, I pray for the entire United States. Humanity and decency seem to be in short supply. And the loss of these vital characteristics spreads quickly. Protect us, Holy One. Empower us to be decent and human, to tell the truth when others aren't, and to create communities of accountability where inhumanity and indecency are not accepted. Amen.[196]

---

195. Mufson, "Trump-appointed regulators reject plan to rescue coal and nuclear plants."

196. Cox, Moyer, and Vargas, "He saw a dazed woman put out in the cold by a Baltimore hospital. He started filming." Four men in uniform, possibly security guards, left a young woman standing by a bus stop wearing only a hospital gown and socks. In the video filmed by Baraka, the woman appears dazed and occasionally crying out. Baraka

Prayers

January 14, 2018

Gracious God, bless Senator Dianne Feinstein. In recent days she released transcripts of testimony shedding light on the Russia investigation, short-circuiting deceptive attempts to undercut the inquiry. She also made a clear, strong statement condemning the Occupant's racism. Grant her continuing wisdom and courage. Allow her honesty and bravery to spur her fellow lawmakers to bold action for the common good. Amen.[197]

January 15, 2018

God of Truth, today we honor Rev. Dr. Martin Luther King Jr. for his leadership in the civil rights movement.

Some people become leaders by offering easy answers, promising quick rewards, scapegoating outsiders, and telling reassuring lies. Rev. Dr. King did none of that. Following him involved personal risk, long-term struggle, refusing hatred, and telling unwelcome truth.

Tonight I give thanks for the many people who chose to follow Rev. Dr. King. The mothers and fathers and neighbors and elders and students and children and workers and teachers and everybody else, too. Bless them and their legacy of strength and solidarity.

Grant the rest of us a portion of their wisdom and bravery as we choose what leaders we follow. Amen.

January 17, 2018

Holy God, I lift up the Israeli organization Rabbis for Human Rights. The prime minister of Israel is planning the expulsion of asylum seekers from Eritrea and Sudan. Rabbis for Human Rights is overseeing the Anne Frank Sanctuary movement, in which people who honor the Jewish tradition of

---

called an ambulance to come back and pick up the woman. The hospital's CEO eventually apologized in a news conference, calling the incident a "breakdown of basic human compassion."

197. Fandos, LaFraniere, and Rosenberg, "Democratic Senator releases transcript of interview with dossier firm." Senator Dianne Feinstein shocked her Republican colleagues on Tuesday, January 9, 2018, by publically presenting an interview transcript that outlined the help given to the Trump campaign. Feinstein stated, "the American people deserve the opportunity to see what he said and judge for themselves."

human rights and the legacy of Anne Frank prepare to hide the African refugees.

There were brave souls who hid Jewish people when they were being rounded up. These faithful Jews are ready to do the same for others. Bless them. May their witness change the political possibilities in Israel.

For the rest of us, God, who read Anne Frank's diary and loved her, imaginatively identifying with this brilliant spirit or those who sheltered her, tune our ears to hear the calls to round up, expel, deport, or keep out those of particular ancestry. May they never pass unnoticed or unremarked. May they always raise red flags and set off alarm bells. Enable us to rise to the occasion and protect our fellows. Amen.[198]

January 19, 2018

Holy God, I pray tonight for every person who manages a household budget, making serious decisions about priorities and values that affect the members of the household and the broader community. Every week, every month, every year, people of good will do all they can to use their financial resources in ways that support, nourish, shelter, and care for their families, broadly defined. This work—at the kitchen table with bills and statements—is unglamorous. There are no news cameras waiting anxiously for results. It's just hard. And when it is done with love, it can also be holy. Bless those who exercise economic wisdom in the service of the common good. Amen.

January 20, 2018

Fierce God, bless all who are participating in Women's Marches this weekend. May we draw strength from our unity and wisdom from our multiplicity. Amen.[199]

---

198. Ballesteros, "Anne Frank Movement: hundreds of rabbis promise to hide African refugees facing deportation in Israel."

199. Mazzei, Fortin, and Piccoli, "Women's March 2018: Protestors take to the streets for the second straight year." For the second year in a row, millions of women took to the street across the country in opposition to Donald Trump and his administration's policies.

Prayers

January 22, 2018

Gracious God, I pray tonight for the Pennsylvania State Supreme Court, which ruled that the congressional district map is an unconstitutional gerrymander that must be redrawn. May their ruling be a decisive step towards functioning democracy. Amen.[200]

January 23, 2018

This time last year I was experiencing constant outrage, indignation, anxiety, and fear. On January 24, 2017, I took up a spiritual discipline of praying for people who were resisting the forces of hatred and greed in our society. I hoped this would encourage me to be—for some portion of the day—in a different attitude about the political realities of the U.S. To be in a space of celebration, encouragement, connection, and positivity. I decided to post these prayers on Facebook as a form of accountability. I didn't manage every day, but the prayer at the bottom of this post will be number 307.

This spiritual exercise took on a life of its own in relation to you, friends both near and far. I am immensely grateful for the ways in which you have prayed with me, sent prayer requests, and been the examples of resistance that have inspired me.

While this discipline has been deeply helpful to me, it is time to pass the torch to someone else. I am delighted that my dear friend and former student, Rev. Joanna Hipp, will be taking over the prayers of resistance. Please follow or friend her to keep the community of prayer going. Know that I will continue to pray for and with all of you.

And for my final prayer in this year-long exercise: God bless the resistance. Amen.

---

200. Gabriel and Wines, "Pennsylvania congressional district map is ruled unconstitutional."

Bibliography

Abbruzzese, Jason. "The Weather Channel wants you to know there's a more pressing issue than the weather right now." *Mashable* (October 20, 2017). https://mashable.com/2017/10/20/weather-channel-puerto-rico-website/#AMVOxDigFsqM.

Abutaleb, Yasmeen and Dane Levine. "Eighteen states sue to block Trump's cut to Obamacare subsidies." *Business Insider* (October 13, 2017). http://www.businessinsider.com/states-sue-trump-obamacare-csr-cut-2017-10.

Adams, Liam and Sam Hoisington. "What major universities had to say about Trump's move to roll back DACA." *The Chronicle of Higher Education* (September 5, 2017). https://www.chronicle.com/article/What-Major-Universities-Had-to/241095.

Adams, Robert Merrihew. "Marilyn McCord Adams obituary." *The Guardian* (March 31, 2017). https://www.theguardian.com/world/2017/mar/31/marilyn-mccord-adams.

Aisch, Gregor, et al. "How France voted." *The New York Times* (May 7, 2017). https://www.nytimes.com/interactive/2017/05/07/world/europe/france-election-results-maps.html.

Anapol, Avery. "Faith leaders write to Senate leadership opposing tax plan." *The Hill* (November 29, 2017). http://thehill.com/homenews/senate/362433-faith-leaders-write-to-senate-leadership-opposing-tax-plan.

———. "Faith leaders write to Senate leadership opposing tax plan." *The Hill* (November 29, 2017). http://thehill.com/homenews/senate/362433-faith-leaders-write-to-senate-leadership-opposing-tax-plan.

Andrade, Chittaranjan and Rajiv Rahakrishnan. "Prayer and healing: A medical and scientific perspective on randomized controlled trials." *Indian Journal of Psychiatry* 51 (Oct–Dec 2009) 247–53. https://www.ncbi.nlm.nih.gov/pmc/articles/PMC2802370/.

Andrews, Travis. "'The President Stole Your Land': Patagonia, REI blast Trump on national monument rollbacks." *The Washington Post* (December 5, 2017). https://www.washingtonpost.com/news/morning-mix/wp/2017/12/05/the-president-stole-your-land-patagonia-rei-blast-trump-on-national-monument-rollbacks/?utm_term=.654840983e13.

Apuzzo, Matt and Emmarie Huetteman. "Sally Yates tells senators she warned Trump about Michael Flynn." *The New York Times* (May 9, 2017). https://www.nytimes.com/2017/05/08/us/politics/michael-flynn-sally-yates-hearing.html.

The Associated Press. "Sixteen Attorneys General sue Trump administration over ending DACA." *WNYC News* (September 6, 2017). https://www.wnyc.org/story/16-attorneys-general-sue-trump-administration-over-ending-daca/.

Bibliography

Astor, Maggie. "Protestors in Durham topple a Confederate monument." *The New York Times* (August 14, 2017). https://www.nytimes.com/2017/08/14/us/protesters-in-durham-topple-a-confederate-monument.html.

Baker, Peter and Eileen Sullivan. "Trump shares inflammatory anti-Muslim videos, and Britain's leader condemns them." *The New York Times* (November 29, 2017). https://www.nytimes.com/2017/11/29/us/politics/trump-anti-muslim-videos-jayda-fransen.html?mtrref=www.google.com.

Ballesteros, Carlos. "Anne Frank Movement: hundreds of rabbis promise to hide African refugees facing deportation in Israel." *Newsweek* (January 17, 2018). http://www.newsweek.com/israel-immigration-refugees-rabbis-anne-frank-deportation-783969.

Belson, Ken. "Kaepernick's protest cascades into protests over his job situation." *The New York Times* (August 23, 2017). https://www.nytimes.com/2017/08/23/sports/football/nfl-protest-colin-kaepernick.html.

Berman, Mark. "As more Jewish facilities get threats, all 100 senators ask Trump administration for 'swift action'." *The Washington Post* (March 7, 2017). https://www.washingtonpost.com/news/post-nation/wp/2017/03/07/as-more-jewish-facilities-get-threats-senators-ask-trump-administration-for-swift-action/.

Berman, Mark and John Wagner. "Why almost every state is partially or fully rebuffing Trump's election commission." *The Washington Post* (July 5, 2017). https://www.washingtonpost.com/news/post-nation/wp/2017/07/05/most-states-are-now-partially-or-fully-refusing-to-hand-over-data-to-trumps-voter-fraud-commission/?utm_term=.8da807bc1ee3.

Bharath, Deepa. "Santa Ana mosque members break Ramadan fast with tacos." *The Orange County Register* (June 4, 2017). https://www.ocregister.com/2017/06/04/indo-chinese-mosque-members-break-ramadan-fast-with-tacos/.

Bidgood, Jess, et al. "Baltimore mayor had statues removed in 'best interest of my city'." *The New York Times* (August 16, 2017). https://www.nytimes.com/2017/08/16/us/baltimore-confederate-statues.html.

Blair, Elizabeth. "Women are speaking up about harassment and abuse, but why now?" *NPR* (October 27, 2017). https://www.npr.org/2017/10/27/560231232/women-are-speaking-up-about-harassment-and-abuse-but-why-now.

Blinder, Alan and Michael Wines. "North Carolina is ordered to redraw its congressional map." *The New York Times.* (January 9, 2018). "https://www.nytimes.com/2018/01/09/us/north-carolina-gerrymander.html.

Bloch, Matthew, et al. "Alabama election results: Doug Jones defeats Roy Moore in U.S. Senate race." *The New York Times* (December 12, 2017). https://www.nytimes.com/elections/results/alabama-senate-special-election-roy-moore-doug-jones.

Bloom, Linda. "Consecration of gay bishop against church law." *United Methodist News Service* (April 28, 2017). http://www.umc.org/news-and-media/consecration-of-gay-bishop-against-church-law.

Bonesteel, Matt and Marissa Payne. "LeBron James sticks up for Stephen Curry, calls President Trump a 'bum'." *The Washington Post* (September 23, 2017). https://www.washingtonpost.com/news/early-lead/wp/2017/09/23/lebron-james-sticks-up-for-stephen-curry-calls-president-trump-a-bum/.

Borchers, Callum. "A reporter broke White House rules by streaming live audio of an off-camera briefing." *The Washington Post* (July 19, 2017). https://www.washingtonpost.

Bibliography

com/news/the-fix/wp/2017/07/19/a-reporter-broke-white-house-rules-by-streaming-live-audio-of-an-off-camera-briefing/?utm_term=.530af1819977.

Bosman, Julie, et al. "Brownback tax cuts set off a revolt by Kansas Republicans." *The New York Times* (June 7, 2017). https://www.nytimes.com/2017/06/07/us/sam-brownback-kansas-budget-override.html.

"The Boston Declaration: A Prophetic Appeal to Christians of the United States." (November 20, 2017). https://thebostondeclaration.com/blog/2017/11/18/the-boston-declaration.

Briscoe, Tony. "Court: Civil Rights Act covers LGBT workplace bias." *Chicago Tribune* (April 4, 2017). http://www.chicagotribune.com/news/local/breaking/ct-law-covers-lgbt-workplace-bias-20170404-story.html

Brueggemann, Walter. *The Prophetic Imagination*. 2nd ed. Minneapolis: Fortress, 2001.

Buchanan, Larry. "What happened in Ferguson?" *The New York Times* (August 10, 2015). https://www.nytimes.com/interactive/2014/08/13/us/ferguson-missouri-town-under-siege-after-police-shooting.html.

Bullock, Tom. "Gerrymandering and recruiting: A candidate ME conversation with Sen. Jackson." *WFAE News* (August 10, 2017). http://wfae.org/post/gerrymandering-and-recruiting-candidate-me-conversation-sen-jackson#stream/0.

Burns, Alexander. "Two federal judges rule against Trump's latest travel ban." *The New York Times* (March 15, 2017). https://www.nytimes.com/2017/03/15/us/politics/trump-travel-ban.html.

Calvin, Jean. *Institutes of the Christian Religion*. Volume II. Translated by Ford Lewis Battles. Philadelphia: Westminster, 1960.

Carman, Tim. "After Maria, Jose Andres and his team have prepared more hot meals in Puerto Rico than the Red Cross." *The Washington Post* (October 18, 2017). https://www.washingtonpost.com/news/food/wp/2017/10/18/post-maria-jose-andres-and-his-team-have-served-more-meals-in-puerto-rico-than-the-red-cross/.

Carroll, Aaron E. "The cost can be debated, but meals on wheels gets results." *The New York Times* (March 17, 2017). https://www.nytimes.com/2017/03/17/upshot/the-cost-can-be-debated-but-meals-on-wheels-gets-results.html.

Chappell, Bill. "Federal judge temporarily blocks deportation of 1,400 Iraqis nationwide." *National Public Radio* (June 27, 2017). https://www.npr.org/sections/thetwo-way/2017/06/27/534547354/federal-judge-blocks-u-s-deportation-of-iraqis-nationwide.

Chavez, Aida. "Jimmy Carter greets every passenger on flight from Atlanta to DC." *The Hill* (June 12, 2017). http://thehill.com/blogs/in-the-know/in-the-know/337381-jimmy-carter-greets-every-passenger-on-flight-from-atlanta.

Christensen, Doreen. "AT&T helps you locate loved ones in Puerto Rico after Hurricane Maria." *The Sun Sentinel* (September 26, 2017). http://www.sun-sentinel.com/features/deals-shopping/sfl-at-t-helps-you-locate-loved-ones-in-puerto-rico-after-hurricane-maria-20170926-story.html.

Cirillo, Chris. "Harvey brings catastrophic floods to Houston; at least five reported dead." *The New York Times* (August 27, 2017). https://www.nytimes.com/2017/08/27/us/harvey-texas-storm.html.

Coscarelli, Joe. "Kellyanne Conway admits 'Bowling Green Massacre' error." *The New York Times* (February 3, 2017). https://www.nytimes.com/2017/02/03/us/politics/bowling-green-massacre-kellyanne-conway.html.

Bibliography

Cox, John Woodrow, et al. "He saw a dazed woman put out in the cold by a Baltimore hospital. He started filming." *The Washington Post* (January 12, 2018). https://www.washingtonpost.com/local/social-media-fury-follows-video-of-dazed-woman-put-out-in-cold-by-baltimore-hospital/2018/01/11/b8a7866c-f70d-11e7-b34a-b85626af34ef_story.html.

Davidson, Joe. "EPA won't be able to do the right thing under Trump, says latest protesting official." *The Washington Post* (August 1, 2017). https://www.washingtonpost.com/news/powerpost/wp/2017/08/01/epa-doing-the-right-thing-is-not-possible-under-trump-says-resigning-official/.

Davis, Aaron C. "D.C. and Maryland sue President Trump, alleging breach of constitutional oath." *The Washington Post* (June 12, 2017). https://www.washingtonpost.com/local/politics/dc-and-maryland-to-sue-president-trump-alleging-breach-of-constitutional-oath.html.

Decker, Cathleen. "At naturalization ceremony and healthcare rally, Kamala Harris goes after Trump and his GOP allies." *The Los Angeles Times* (July 3, 2017). http://www.latimes.com/politics/essential/la-pol-ca-essential-politics-updates-sen-kamala-harris-goes-after-president-1499118802-htmlstory.html.

Dennis, Brady. "In the heart of coal country, EPA gets an earful about Clean Power Plan's fate." *The Washington Post* (November 28, 2017). https://www.washingtonpost.com/news/energy-environment/wp/2017/11/28/in-the-heart-of-coal-country-epa-gets-an-earful-about-clean-power-plans-fate/?utm_term=.8caa80dbfaf3.

Doucleff, Michaeleen. "Fetal cells may protect mom from disease long after the baby's born." *National Public Radio* (October 26, 2015). https://www.npr.org/sections/health-shots/2015/10/26/449966350/fetal-cells-may-protect-mom-from-disease-long-after-the-babys-born.

Duca, Lauren. "Donald Trump is gaslighting America." *Teen Vogue* (December 10, 2016). https://www.teenvogue.com/story/donald-trump-is-gaslighting-america.

Dunlap, Matthew. "I'm on Trump's voter fraud commission. I'm suing it to find out what it's doing." *The Washington Post* (November 30, 2017). https://www.washingtonpost.com/outlook/im-on-trumps-voter-fraud-commission-im-suing-it-to-find-out-what-its-doing/2017/11/30/1034574c-d3b0-11e7-95bf-df7c19270879_story.html?utm_term=.6b85e8d4d1b1.

Dwyer, Colin. "Boston students get a glimpse of a whole new world, with different maps." *National Public Radio* (March 21, 2017). https://www.npr.org/sections/thetwo-way/2017/03/21/520938221/boston-students-get-a-glimpse-of-a-whole-new-world-with-different-maps.

Dwyer, Dialynn. "Rep. Joe Kennedy calls GOP health care repeal bill an 'act of malice.'" *Boston.com* (March 9, 2017). https://www.boston.com/news/politics/2017/03/09/rep-joe-kennedy-calls-gop-health-care-repeal-bill-an-act-of-malice.

The Editorial Board. "Welcoming transgender Boy Scouts." *The New York Times* (February 2, 2017). https://www.nytimes.com/2017/02/02/opinion/welcoming-transgender-boy-scouts.html.

The Editorial Board. "Will Trump's lows ever hit rock bottom?" *USA Today* (December 12, 2017). https://www.usatoday.com/story/opinion/2017/12/12/trump-lows-ever-hit-rock-bottom-editorials-debates/945947001/.

The Editors of GQ. "Colin Kaepernick is GQ's 2017 Citizen of the Year." *GQ* (November 13, 2017). https://www.gq.com/story/colin-kaepernick-cover-men-of-the-year.

Bibliography

Elk, Mike. "Harry Belafonte tells crowd at likely last public appearance: 'We Shall Overcome.'" *The Guardian* (October 21, 2017). https://www.theguardian.com/us-news/2017/oct/21/harry-belafonte-we-shall-overcome-trump.

Eschman, Todd. "Eight-year-old Cahokia football players take a knee for national anthem." *Belleville News-Democrat* (September 18, 2017). http://www.bnd.com/sports/article173934311.html.

Etman, Omar. "Thousands counter-protest 'Free Speech' rally in Boston." *PBS News Hour* (August 19, 2017). https://www.pbs.org/newshour/nation/thousands-counter-protest-free-speech-rally-boston.

Fandos, Nicholas, et al. "Democratic senator releases transcript of interview with dossier firm." *The New York Times* (January 9, 2018). https://www.nytimes.com/2018/01/09/us/politics/feinstein-fusion-gps-glenn-simpson-transcript.html.

Fandos, Nicholas. "Climate March draws thousands of protesters alarmed by Trump's environmental agenda." *The New York Times* (April 29, 2017). https://www.nytimes.com/2017/04/29/us/politics/peoples-climate-march-trump.html.

Fausset, Richard. "North Carolina strikes a deal to repeal restrictive bathroom law." *The New York Times* (March 29, 2017). https://www.nytimes.com/2017/03/29/us/north-carolina-lawmakers-reach-deal-to-repeal-so-called-bathroom-bill.html.

Fears, Darryl. "For a few hours, Badlands National Park was bad to the bone in defiance of Trump." *The Washington Post* (January 24, 2017). https://www.washingtonpost.com/news/energy-environment/wp/2017/01/24/for-a-few-hours-badlands-national-parks-was-bad-to-the-bone-in-defiance-of-trump/?utm_term=.3b3a8db1d75e.

Fernandez, Manny. "Federal judge blocks Texas' ban on 'Sanctuary Cities.'" *The New York Times* (August 30, 2017). https://www.nytimes.com/2017/08/30/us/judge-texas-sanctuary-cities.html.

Figueroa, Ariana. "Mainland colleges offer in-state tuition to students affected by Hurricane Maria." *National Public Radio* (October 22, 2017). https://www.npr.org/sections/ed/2017/10/22/558353633/mainland-colleges-offer-in-state-tuition-to-students-affected-by-hurricane-maria.

Fountain, Henry. "A total solar eclipse leaves a nation in awe." *The New York Times* (August 21, 2017). https://www.nytimes.com/2017/08/21/science/total-solar-eclipse-day.html?login=email&auth=login-email.

Friedman, Lisa. "Court blocks E.P.A. effort to suspend Obama-era methane rule." *The New York Times* (July 3, 2017). https://www.nytimes.com/2017/07/03/climate/court-blocks-epa-effort-to-suspend-obama-era-methane-rule.html.

Gabriel, Trip and Michael Wines. "Pennsylvania Congressional District Map is Ruled Unconstitutional." *The New York Times* (January 22, 2018). https://www.nytimes.com/2018/01/22/us/pennsylvania-maps-congress.html.

Gettleman, Jeffrey. "State Dept. dissent cable on Trump's ban draws, 1,000 signatures." *The New York Times* (January 31, 2017). https://www.nytimes.com/2017/01/31/world/americas/state-dept-dissent-cable-trump-immigration-order.html.

Gibbons-Neff, Thomas. "Despite Trump announcement, Coast Guard will not 'break faith' with transgender troops." *The Washington Post* (August 1, 2017). https://www.washingtonpost.com/news/checkpoint/wp/2017/08/01/despite-trump-announcement-coast-guard-will-not-break-faith-with-transgender-troops/?utm_term=.8c3afe1cfa7d

Bibliography

Gillespie, Lisa. "Grawemeyer winner on links between 'The Cross And The Lynching Tree'." *WFPL News* (November 30, 2017). http://wfpl.org/grawemeyer-winner-on-links-between-the-cross-and-the-lynching-tree/.

Gladstone, Rick and Mark Lander. "Defying Tump, U.N. General Assembly condemns U.S. decree on Jerusalem." *The New York Times* (December 21, 2017). https://www.nytimes.com/2017/12/21/world/middleeast/trump-jerusalem-united-nations.html.

Goldstein, Joseph. "Eric Garner's 27-year-old daughter is in a coma." *The New York Times* (December 25, 2017). https://www.nytimes.com/2017/12/25/nyregion/eric-garners-27-year-old-daughter-is-in-a-coma.html.

Goodstein, Laurie. "Welcome refugees, churches say in public challenge to Trump." *The New York Times* (March 2, 2017). https://www.nytimes.com/2017/03/02/us/churches-welcome-refugees-trump.html.

Goodstein, Laurie, et al. "Trump administration rolls back birth control mandate." *The New York Times* (October 6, 2017). https://www.nytimes.com/2017/10/06/us/politics/trump-contraception-birth-control.html.

Green, Erica L. "Bethune-Cookman graduates greet Betsy De Vos with turned backs." *The New York Times* (May 10, 2017). https://www.nytimes.com/2017/05/10/us/politics/betsy-devos-bethune-cookman-commencement.html.

Grygiel, Chris. "Washington, other states seek hearing on latest Trump travel ban." *The Seattle Times* (March 13, 2017). https://www.seattletimes.com/seattle-news/northwest/washington-other-states-sue-again-seek-fast-hearing-on-trump-travel-ban-20/.

Guadalupe, Patricia and Marissa Armas. "'Do the right thing': Thousands rally in D.C. for Dream Act to protect young immigrants." *NBC News* (December 6, 2017). https://www.nbcnews.com/news/latino/do-right-thing-thousands-rally-d-c-dream-act-protect-n827131.

"Habitat for Humanity prepares long-term recovery plan for Puerto Rico." *Habitat for Humanity News Release* (October 3, 2017). https://www.habitat.org/newsroom/2017/habitat-humanity-prepares-long-term-hurricane-recovery-plan-puerto-rico.

Hallesby, O. *Prayer*. Translated by Clarence J. Carlsen. Minneapolis: Augsburg, 1994.

Hallinan, Bridget. "JetBlue launches hurricane relief plan for Puerto Rico." *Condé Nast* (September 28, 2017). https://www.cntraveler.com/story/jetblue-launches-hurricane-relief-plan-for-puerto-rico.

Hansen, Piper and Olivia Dawson. "Black Student Union holds sit-in." *Manual RedEye* (November 14, 2017). http://manualredeye.com/2017/11/14/black-student-union-holds-sit/.

Harak, G. Simon. *Virtuous Passions: The Formation of Christian Character*. Eugene, OR: Wipf & Stock, 1993.

Hawkins, Derek. "Trump vs. Trump, again: Judge cites presidential tweets as he blocks DACA phaseout." *The Washington Post* (January 10, 2018). https://www.washingtonpost.com/news/morning-mix/wp/2018/01/10/trump-vs-trump-again-judge-cites-presidential-tweets-as-he-blocks-daca-phaseout/.

Heim, Joe. "Standing Rock Sioux tribe will lead Indian march on Washington." *The Washington Post* (March 7, 2017). https://www.washingtonpost.com/local/standing-rock-sioux-tribe-leads-indian-march-on-washington/2017/03/07/.

Heschel, Susannah. "Their feet were praying: Remembering the inspiration Heschel and King drew from each other." *The New York Jewish Week* (January 10, 2012). http://jewishweek.timesofisrael.com/their-feet-were-praying/.

Bibliography

Hirschfeld Davis, Julie. "Trump mocks Warren as 'Pocahontas' at Navajo Veterans' event." *The New York Times* (November 27, 2017). https://www.nytimes.com/2017/11/27/us/politics/trump-elizabeth-warren-pocahontas-navajo.html.

Hirschfield Davis, Julie and Michael M. Grynbaum. "Trump intensifies his attacks on journalists and condemns F.B.I. 'leakers.'" *The New York Times* (February 24, 2017). https://www.nytimes.com/2017/02/24/us/politics/white-house-sean-spicer-briefing.html.

Horowitz, Jason. "Pope criticizes climate change deniers and Trump on DACA." *The New York Times* (September 11, 2017). https://www.nytimes.com/2017/09/11/world/europe/pope-climate-daca-trump-colombia.html.

Horwitz, Sari, et al. "Sessions orders Justice Department to review all police reform agreements." *The Washington Post* (April 3, 2017). https://www.washingtonpost.com/world/national-security/sessions-orders-justice-department-to-review-all-police-reform-agreements/2017/04/03/ba934058-18bd-11e7-9887-1a5314b56a08_story.html?utm_term=.f43a787ca11c.

Horton, Alex. "An elephant was stranded nine miles out to sea. Then the Sri Lankan Navy arrived." *The Washington Post* (July 13, 2017). https://www.washingtonpost.com/news/animalia/wp/2017/07/13/an-elephant-was-stranded-9-miles-out-to-sea-then-the-sri-lanka-navy-arrived/.

Hsu, Tiffany. "F.C.C. plan to roll back net neutrality worries small businesses." *The New York Times* (November 22, 2017). https://www.nytimes.com/2017/11/22/business/net-neutrality-small-businesses.html.

Itkowitz, Colby. "'Every person deserves to rest in peace' American Muslims raising money to repair vandalized Jewish cemetery." *The Washington Post* (February 21, 2017). https://www.washingtonpost.com/news/inspired-life/wp/2017/02/21/every-person-deserves-to-rest-in-peace-american-muslims-raising-money-to-repair-vandalized-jewish-cemetery/?utm_term=.f164b5f8710d.

Japsen, Bruce. "AMA says McConnell's Trumpcare bill violates 'do no harm' principle." *Forbes* (June 26, 2017). https://www.forbes.com/sites/brucejapsen/2017/06/26/ama-says-mcconnells-trumpcare-bill-violates-do-no-harm-principle/#1361f8744040.

Jenkins, Aric. "White nationalists hold 'White Lives Matter' rallies in Tennessee." *Time* (October 28, 2017). http://time.com/5001532/white-lives-matter-rally-murfreesboro/.

Johnson, Eliana. "Kennedy stays quiet on whether he'll retire at end of Supreme Court term." *Politico* (June 25, 2017). https://www.politico.com/story/2017/06/25/justice-kennedy-retire-supreme-court-239940.

Johnson, Jenna and Adam Entous. "Trump notes new national security list 'in play' after first choice turns down offer." *The Washington Post* (February 17, 2017). https://www.washingtonpost.com/news/post-politics/wp/2017/02/16/trumps-pick-to-replace-michael-flynn-as-national-security-adviser-turns-down-offer-people-familiar-with-decision-say-2/?utm_term=.16233edafbof.

Johnson, Kevin C. "U2, Ed Sheeran cancel St. Louis concerts; other events also called off." *St. Louis Post-Dispatch* (September 17, 2017). http://www.stltoday.com/news/local/crime-and-courts/u-ed-sheeran-cancel-st-louis-concerts-other-events-also/article_983bf92a-a96e-56d1-8304-cffa69ee5821.html.

Kane, Paul and Ed O'Keefe. "Republicans vote to rebuke Elizabeth Warren, saying she impugned Sessions's character." *The Washington Post* (February 8, 2017). https://www.

Bibliography

washingtonpost.com/news/powerpost/wp/2017/02/07/republicans-vote-to-rebuke-elizabeth-warren-for-impugning-sessionss-character/?utm_term=.0e96260e5029.

Kaplan, Thomas. "Health care overhaul collapses as two Republican Senators defect." *The New York Times* (July 17, 2017). https://www.nytimes.com/2017/07/17/us/politics/health-care-overhaul-collapses-as-two-republican-senators-defect.html.

Kaplan, Thomas and Robert Pear. "Health bill appears dead as pivotal GOP Senator declares opposition." *The New York Times* (September 25, 2017). https://www.nytimes.com/2017/09/25/us/politics/obamacare-repeal-susan-collins-dead.html.

Kenning, Chris. "Hundreds of protesters rally outside Pence speech: 'Save our care.'" *The Courier Journal* (March 11, 2017). https://www.courier-journal.com/story/news/politics/2017/03/11/protesters-gather-before-pence-speech/99015880/.

———. "Louisville pro-immigration rally draws 5,000." *The Courier-Journal* (January 30, 2017). https://www.courier-journal.com/story/news/local/2017/01/30/4-things-know-pro-immigration-rally/97234970/.

Korosec, Kirsten. "Tesla is helping Puerto Rico get power after Hurricane Maria." *Fortune* (September 28, 2017). http://fortune.com/2017/09/28/tesla-battery-puerto-rico-power/.

Kraker, Dan. "At Line 3 Pipeline hearing, it's environment vs. jobs." *MPRN News* (September 28, 2017). https://www.mprnews.org/story/2017/09/28/enbridge-line-3-opponents-rally-capitol-before-hearing.

Kramer, Elizabeth. "Actors 'Angels in America' takes flight—review." *The Courier-Journal* (September 1, 2017). https://www.courier-journal.com/story/entertainment/theater/2017/09/01/actors-angels-america-takes-flight-review/613585001/.

Landler, Mark. "Merkel meets Trump, the defender versus the disrupter." *The New York Times* (March 17, 2017). https://www.nytimes.com/2017/03/17/world/europe/angela-merkel-donald-trump.html.

———. "Trump recognizes Jerusalem as Israel's capital and orders U.S. embassy to move." *The New York Times* (December 5, 2017). https://www.nytimes.com/2017/12/06/world/middleeast/trump-jerusalem-israel-capital.html.

Landler, Mark and David Sanger. "Trump to force congress to act on Iran nuclear deal." *The New York Times* (October 5, 2017). https://www.nytimes.com/2017/10/05/world/middleeast/trump-iran-nuclear-deal.html.

Lee, Traci G. "10 resign from President's Advisory Commission on Asian Americans and Pacific Islanders." *NBCnews*. (February 16, 2017). https://www.nbcnews.com/news/asian-america/10-resign-from-president-s-advisory-commission-on-asian-americans-pacific-islanders-n721386.

Lee, Yen Nee. "'The President stole your land.' outdoor gear company Patagonia takes a big swing at Trump." *CNBC News* (December 4, 2017). https://www.cnbc.com/2017/12/04/the-president-stole-your-land-outdoor-gear-company-patagonia-takes-a-big-swing-at-trump.html.

Leonnig, Carol, et al. "Special Counsel Mueller using grand jury in federal court in Washington as part of Russia investigation." *The Washington Post* (August 3, 2017). https://www.washingtonpost.com/politics/special-counsel-mueller-using-grand-jury-in-federal-court-in-washington-as-part-of-russia-investigation/2017/08/03/15 85da56–7887-11e7–8f39-eeb7d3a2d304_story.html?utm_term=.1efe5fbf76f4.

Link, Taylor. "Sen. Sherrod Brown: Steve Bannon is a 'white supremacist.'" *Salon* (October 22, 2017). https://www.salon.com/2017/10/22/sherrod-brown-agrees-that-steve-bannon-is-a-white-supremacist/.

Bibliography

Liptak, Adam. "Court refuses to reinstate travel ban, dealing Trump another legal loss." *The New York Times* (February 9, 2017). https://www.nytimes.com/2017/02/09/us/politics/appeals-court-trump-travel-ban.html.

Maheshwari, Sapna. "Super Bowl commercials feature political undertones and celebrity cameos." *The New York Times* (February 5, 2017). https://www.nytimes.com/2017/02/05/business/media/commercials-super-bowl-51.html.

Markon, Jerry, et.al. "Judge halts deportations as refugee ban causes worldwide furor." *The Washington Post* (January 29, 2017). https://www.washingtonpost.com/local/social-issues/refugees-detained-at-us-airports-challenge-trumps-executive-order/2017/01/28/e69501a2-e562-11e6-a547-5fb9411d332c_story.html?utm_term=.fdd0ea5733e3.

Martin, Jonathan and Alexander Burns. "Republican Senator vital to health bill's passage won't support it." *The New York Times* (June 23, 2017). https://www.nytimes.com/2017/06/23/us/politics/health-care-bill-senate.html.

Mather, Victor. "First woman to enter Boston Marathon runs it again, 50 years later." *The New York Times* (April 17, 2017). https://www.nytimes.com/2017/04/17/sports/boston-marathon-kathrine-switzer.html.

Mazzei, Patricia, et al. "Women's March 2018: protestors take to the streets for the second straight year." *The New York Times* (January 20, 2018). https://www.nytimes.com/2018/01/20/us/womens-march.html.

McAuley, James. "They were aided by Portugal's 'Schindler,' Now these WWII refugees are trying to help others." *The Washington Post* (July2, 2017). https://www.washingtonpost.com/world/europe/they-were-aided-by-frances-schindler-now-these-world-war-ii-refugees-are-trying-to-help-others/2017/07/01/fbe53200–5a8a-11e7-aa69–3964a7d55207_story.html.

McCord Adams, Marilyn. "Prayer as the 'Lifeline of Theology.'" *Anglican Theological Review* 98 (2016) 272.

McDonogh, Pat. "DACA supporters rally at federal courthouse after order rescinded." *The Courier-Journal* (September 5, 2017). https://www.courier-journal.com/picture-gallery/news/local/2017/09/05/daca-supporters-rally-at-federal-courthouse-after-order-rescinded/105292014/.

McFadden, Robert D. "Edith Windsor, whose same-sex marriage fight let to landmark ruling, dies at 88." *The New York Times* (September 12, 2017). https://www.nytimes.com/2017/09/12/us/edith-windsor-dead-same-sex-marriage-doma.html.

McKenzie, Linday. "Three professors are fasting to protest their university's 'silence' on the travel ban." *The Chronicle of Higher Education* (February 6, 2017). https://www.chronicle.com/article/3-Professors-Are-Fasting-to/239133.

Mettler, Katie. "Francisca Lino, mom of six, is about to be deported. Her congressman protested and was handcuffed." *The Washington Post* (March 14, 2017). https://www.washingtonpost.com/news/morning-mix/wp/2017/03/14/francisca-lino-mom-of-six-is-about-to-be-deported-in-protest-her-congressman-was-handcuffed/.

———. "Rip currents swept away a Florida family. Then beachgoers formed a human chain." *The Washington Post* (July 11, 2017). https://www.washingtonpost.com/news/morning-mix/wp/2017/07/11/a-riptide-swept-away-a-florida-family-then-beachgoers-formed-a-human-chain/.

———. "This union ironworker wants Paul Ryan's job. He's got a great ad but a losing record." *The Washington Post* (June 21, 2017). https://www.washingtonpost.com/

Bibliography

news/morning-mix/wp/2017/06/21/this-union-ironworker-wants-paul-ryans-job-hes-got-a-great-ad-but-a-losing-record/.

Migliore, Daniel. *Faith Seeking Understanding: An Introduction to Christian Theology.* 3rd edition. Grand Rapids: Eerdmans, 2014.

Modisett, Cara. "Carillon plays 'Lift Every Voice and Sing' as Richard Spencer speaks in Florida." *The Episcopal Cafe* (October 20, 2017). https://www.episcopalcafe.com/carillon-plays-lift-every-voice-and-sing-as-richard-spencer-speaks-in-florida/.

Molteni, Megan. "Diehard coders just rescued NASA's earth science data." *Wired* (February 13, 2017). https://www.wired.com/2017/02/diehard-coders-just-saved-nasas-earth-science-data/.

Montgomery, David, et al. "Gunman kills at least 26 in attack on rural Texas church." *The New York Times* (November 5, 2017). https://www.nytimes.com/2017/11/05/us/church-shooting-texas.html.

Moore, Jack. "Israeli tends refuse to serve in military, take part in occupation." *Newsweek* (December 28, 2017). http://www.newsweek.com/israeli-teens-refuse-serve-military-take-part-occupation-west-bank-761277.

Morin, Amy. "Seven scientifically proven benefits of gratitude that will motivate you to give thanks year-round." *Forbes* (November 23, 2014). https://www.health.harvard.edu/newsletter_article/in-praise-of-gratitude.

Mufson, Steven. "Trump-appointed regulators reject plan to rescue coal and nuclear plants." *The Washington Post* (January 8, 2018). https://www.washingtonpost.com/news/energy-environment/wp/2018/01/08/trump-appointed-regulators-reject-plan-to-rescue-coal-and-nuclear-plants/?utm_term=.945696f0282f.

Muhammad, Ibtihaj. "Ibtihaj Muhammad: I fear President Trump's 'campaign of terror' against American ideals." *Time* (March 20, 2017). http://time.com/4706627/olympic-fencer-ibtihaj-muhammad-donald-trump/.

Newcomb, Alyssa. "The backlash is building over the plan to gut net neutrality." *NBC News* (November 22, 2017). https://www.nbcnews.com/tech/tech-news/backlash-building-over-plan-gut-net-neutrality-n823436.

Nixon, Ron. "Coast Guard still supports transgender troops, commandant says." *The New York Times* (August 1, 2017). https://www.nytimes.com/2017/08/01/us/politics/coast-guard-commandant-general-zukunft-transgender-troops.html.

O'Neil, Tim and Mitch Smith. "Former St. Louis officer, Jason Stockley, acquitted in shooting of black driver." *The New York Times* (September 15, 2017). https://www.nytimes.com/2017/09/15/us/jason-stockley-anthony-lamar-smith-st-louis-officer.html.

Ogle, Michelle. "Six members of the Presidential Council on HIV/Aids resign." Interviewed by Steve Inskeep, *National Public Radio* (June 20, 2017). https://www.npr.org/2017/06/20/533617483/6-members-of-the-presidential-advisory-council-on-hiv-aids-resign.

Parker, Ashley and Courtney Teague. "Trump proves an eager tourist in Hawaii, but protesters have 'no aloha for him.'" *The Washington Post* (November 4, 2017). https://www.washingtonpost.com/politics/trump-proves-an-eager-tourist-in-hawaii-but-protesters-have-no-aloha-for-him/2017/11/04/bd059bb6-c127-11e7-959c-fe2b598d8c00_story.html?utm_term=.d06e1401f6e7.

Pazmino, Gloria. "At sanctuary cities gathering, policymakers vow to become Trump's 'worst nightmare.'" *Politico* (March 27, 2017). https://www.politico.com/states/new-

Bibliography

york/city-hall/story/2017/03/at-sanctuary-cities-gathering-policymakers-vow-to-become-trumps-worst-nightmare-110738.

Pear, Robert and Thomas Kaplan. "Senate Republicans unveil new health bill, but divisions remain." *The New York Times* (July 13, 2017). https://www.nytimes.com/2017/07/13/us/politics/senate-republican-health-care-bill.html.

Philipps, Dave. "Judge block's Trump's ban on transgender troops in military." *The New York Times* (October 30, 2017). https://www.nytimes.com/2017/10/30/us/military-transgender-ban.html.

Phillips, Kristine. "In message of defiance to Trump, lawmakers vote to make California a sanctuary state." *The Washington Post* (September 16, 2017). https://www.washingtonpost.com/news/politics/wp/2017/09/16/in-message-of-defiance-to-trump-lawmakers-vote-to-make-california-a-sanctuary-state/.

———. "Mike Pence's Colorado neighbors troll him with a 'Make America Gay Again' banner." *The Washington Post* (December 30, 2017). https://www.washingtonpost.com/news/politics/wp/2017/12/30/mike-pences-colorado-neighbors-troll-him-with-a-make-america-gay-again-banner/?utm_term=.b6169841fe01.

———. "This Democratic senator's thoughts on Trump? We can't write it here." *The Washington Post* (June 10, 2017). https://www.washingtonpost.com/news/the-fix/wp/2017/06/10/this-democratic-senators-thoughts-on-trump-we-cant-write-it-here/.

Pierce, Kent. "Medical supplies heading to Puerto Rico 'con amor.'" *Sun Sentinel* (September 27, 2017). http://www.sun-sentinel.com/features/deals-shoppng/sfl-at-t-helps-you-locate-loved-ones-in-puerto-rico-after-hurricane-maria-20170926-story.html.

Pogrebin, Robin. "16 members of White House Arts Committee resign to protest Trump." *The New York Times* (August 18, 2017). https://www.nytimes.com/2017/08/18/arts/white-house-arts-committee-resigns.html.

Popoich, Nadja and Tatiana Schlossberg. "How cities and states reacted to Trump's decision to exit the Paris climate deal." *The New York Times* (June 2, 2017). https://www.nytimes.com/interactive/2017/06/02/climate/trump-paris-mayors.html.

Price, Edward. "I didn't think I'd ever leave the CIA. But because of Trump, I quit." *The Washington Post* (February 20, 2117). https://www.washingtonpost.com/opinions/i-didnt-think-id-ever-leave-the-cia-but-because-of-trump-i-quit/2017/02/20/fd7aac3e-f456-11e6-b9c9-e83fce42fb6_story.html?utm_term=.bb1c26350868.

Rahner, Karl. *Foundations of Christian Faith: An Introduction to the Idea of Christianity*. Translated by William V. Dych. New York: Crossroad, 1994.

Rank, Barbara. "Letter: Why should I pay indeed?" *Telegraph Herald* (May 12, 2017). "http://www.telegraphherald.com/news/public_announcements/article_824b24ac-3dbf-5390-8cf3-0c4a17b76dbb.html.

Rank, David. "Why I resigned from the Foreign Service after 27 years." *The Washington Post* (June 23, 2017). https://www.washingtonpost.com/opinions/why-i-resigned-from-the-foreign-service-after-27-years/2017/06/23/.

Ransom, Jan and Cristela Guerra. "Hundreds gather in Copley to 'stand up for science.'" *The Boston Globe* (February 19, 2017). https://www.bostonglobe.com/metro/2017/02/19/hundreds-expected-gather-noon-boston-stand-for-science/JVIHjU86mzRkyz2emeLTLN/story.html.

Raphelson, Samantha. "The Merriam-Webster Dictionary has been trolling Trump on Twitter for months." *National Public Radio* (January 26, 2017). https://www.npr.

Bibliography

org/sections/alltechconsidered/2017/01/26/511694558/the-merriam-webster-dictionary-has-been-trolling-trump-for-months.

Rappeport, Alan, and Thomas Kaplan. "Tax bill thrown into uncertainty as first G.O.P senator comes out against it." *The New York Times* (November 15, 2017). https://www.nytimes.com/2017/11/15/us/politics/senate-house-tax-cut.html.

Rather, Dan. *News and Guts*. https://www.facebook.com/newsandguts/.

Robbins, Liz. "'Sanctuary City' mayors vow to defy Trump's immigration order." *The New York Times* (January 25, 2017). https://www.nytimes.com/2017/01/25/nyregion/outraged-mayors-vow-to-defy-trumps-immigration-order.html.

Robertson, Joe. "God Privilege? Kansas City preparing to host the national White Privilege Conference." *The Kansas City Star* (April 3, 2017). http://www.kansascity.com/news/local/article142415794.html.

Rogin, Josh. "John McCain on Comey firing: 'There will be more shoes to drop.'" *The Washington Post* (May 10, 2017). https://www.washingtonpost.com/news/josh-rogin/wp/2017/05/10/john-mccain-on-comey-firing-there-will-be-more-shoes-to-drop/?utm_term=.3ae4952ba1f3.

Rosenberg, Eli. "Protest grows 'out of nowhere' at Kennedy Airport after Iraqis are detained." *The New York Times* (January 28, 2017). https://www.nytimes.com/2017/01/28/nyregion/jfk-protests-trump-refugee-ban.html.

Rubin, Alissa J. "Trump may have pushed Dutch voters away from populism" *The New York Times* (March 16, 2017). https://www.nytimes.com/2017/03/16/world/europe/dutch-election-geert-wilders-europe.html.

Rucker, Philip. "Trump punches back at Flake and Corker, claims a 'love fest' of support in senate." *The Washington Post* (October 24, 2017). https://www.washingtonpost.com/news/post-politics/wp/2017/10/25/trump-punches-back-at-flake-and-corker-claims-a-love-fest-of-support-in-senate/.

"Russia 'tried to hijack US election,' says US senator." *BBC News* (March 31, 2017). http://www.bbc.com/news/world-us-canada-39442901.

Saliers, Don E. *The Soul in Paraphrase*. New York: Seabury, 1980.

Sample, Ian. "We are all made of stars: Half our bodies' atoms 'formed beyond the Milky Way.'" *The Guardian* (July 26, 2017). https://www.theguardian.com/science/2017/jul/27/we-are-all-made-of-stars-half-our-bodies-atoms-formed-beyond-the-milky-way.

Savage, Charlie. "Trump nominee who wrote Bush-era torture memo is scrutinized." *The New York Times* (July 28, 2017). https://www.nytimes.com/2017/06/28/us/politics/trump-nominee-steven-bradbury-bush-era-torture-memos.html.

Segarra, Lisa Marie. "Connecticut NBC affiliate will not air Megyn Kelly's Alex Jones Interview." *Time* (June 17, 2017). http://time.com/4822661/megyn-kelly-alex-jones-interview-nbc-connecticut-wvit/.

Selk, Avi. "A teacher's decision to be 'visibly queer' in his photo with President Trump." *The Washington Post* (June 17, 2017). https://www.washingtonpost.com/news/education/wp/2017/06/17/a-teachers-decision-to-be-visibly-queer-in-his-photo-with-president-trump/.

Sharman, Jon. "Pilots stop 222 asylum seekers being deported from Germany by refusing to fly." *Independent* (December 5, 2017). https://www.independent.co.uk/news/world/europe/german-pilots-refuse-deport-asylum-seekers-lufthansa-angela-merkel-migrants-a8092276.html.

Bibliography

Slavitt, Andy. "The Senate's three tools on health care: Sabotage, speed, and secrecy." *The Washington Post* (June 10, 2017). https://www.washingtonpost.com/opinions/the-senates-three-tools-on-health-care-sabotage-speed-and-secrecy/2017/06/10/11bad38e-4d5a-11e7-9669-250d0b15f83b_story.html.

Sloan, Gene. "Cruise lines extend aid to hard-hit Caribbean islands." *USA Today* (September 28, 2017). https://www.usatoday.com/story/travel/cruises/2017/09/28/cruise-lines-extend-aid-hard-hit-caribbean-islands/708458001/.

Smith, Mitch. "Illinois attorney general sues Chicago over police practices." *The New York Times* (August 29, 2017). https://www.nytimes.com/2017/08/29/us/chicago-police-consent-decree.html.

Somashekhar, Sandhya. "Chicago sues Justice Department over new police grant rules targeting sanctuary cities." *The Washington Post* (August 7, 2017). https://www.washingtonpost.com/news/post-nation/wp/2017/08/07/chicago-to-sue-justice-department-over-new-police-grant-rules-targeting-sanctuary-cities/.

———. "Oregon approves sweeping bill expanding abortion access." *The Washington Post* (August 1, 2017). https://www.washingtonpost.com/news/post-nation/wp/2017/08/15/oregon-approves-sweeping-bill-expanding-abortion-access/.

"Speaker John Bercow defend his comments on Donald Trump." *BBC News* (February 7, 2017). http://www.bbc.com/news/uk-politics-38889941.

Spensley, Allie and Isabel Ting. "U. launches Princeton and Slavery website." *The Daily Princetonian* (November 6, 2017). http://www.dailyprincetonian.com/article/2017/11/princeton-and-slavery-website-launches.

St. Fleur, Nicholas. "Scientists and activists look beyond the March for Science." *The New York Times* (April 17, 2017). https://www.nytimes.com/2017/04/17/science/march-for-science-april-22.html.

Stack, Liam. "Notre Dame students walk out of Mike Pence commencement address." *The New York Times* (May 21, 2017). https://www.nytimes.com/2017/05/21/us/mike-pence-notre-dame-commencement-address.html.

Stein, Perry. "Disability advocates arrested during health care protest at McConnell's office." *The Washington Post* (June 22, 2017). https://www.washingtonpost.com/local/public-safety/disability-advocates-arrested-during-health-care-protest-at-mcconnells-office/2017/06/22/f5dd9992-576f-11e7-ba90-f5875b7d1876_story.html?utm_term=.3226dac76c01.

———. "Richard Spencer hosted an event at a Maryland farm. Halfway through, everyone was kicked out." *The Washington Post* (November 21, 2017). https://www.washingtonpost.com/local/richard-spencer-hosted-an-event-at-a-maryland-farm-halfway-through-everyone-was-kicked-out/2017/11/21/1cd92dfe-9f33-40c4-b6f5-a271a8874c5d_story.html?utm_term=.a983123e6615.

Stein, Perry and Julie Zauzmer. "Dueling clergy protests over the Trump presidency converge on Washington." *The Washington Post* (August 28, 2017). https://www.washingtonpost.com/news/acts-of-faith/wp/2017/08/28/religious-leaders-gather-in-washington-to-show-unified-moral-opposition-to-trump/.

Stolberg, Sheryl Gay and Brian Rosenthal. "Man charged after white nationalist rally in Charlottesville ends in deadly violence." *The New York Times* (August 12, 2017). https://www.nytimes.com/2017/08/12/us/charlottesville-protest-white-nationalist.html.

Sullivan, Sean, Juliet Eilperin, and Dan Balz. "White House launches aggressive push to flip GOP governors opposed to Senate health bill." *The Washington Post* (July 14,

Bibliography

2017). https://www.washingtonpost.com/powerpost/kasich-joins-ranks-of-gop-governors-opposed-to-new-senate-health-bill/2017/07/14/1b158842-68a4-11e7-a1d7-9a32c91c6f40_story.html.

Sullivan, Sean, Juliet Eilperin, and Kelsey Snell. "New health-care plan stumbles under opposition from governors." *The Washington Post* (September 19, 2017). https://www.washingtonpost.com/powerpost/renewed-obamacare-repeal-effort-dealt-a-blow-as-governors-come-out-in-opposition/2017/09/19/499478fe-9d51-11e7-9083-fbfddf6804c2_story.html.

Sullivan, Sean, Michael Scherer, and Paul Kane. "National Republican move against Roy Moore grows—but key Alabama Republicans are not joining in." *The Washington Post* (November 14, 2017). https://www.washingtonpost.com/powerpost/paul-ryan-joins-gop-calls-for-roy-moore-to-end-campaign-amid-sexual-misconduct-allegations/2017/11/14/65a4c824-c951-11e7-aa96-54417592cf72_story.html?utm_term=.748a416615fd.

Tate, Curtis. "McConnell goes back to his hometown and finds surly voters." *The Lexington Herald Leader* (February 22, 2107). http://www.kentucky.com/news/politics-government/article134345014.html.

Thompson, Deanna. *The Virtual Body of Christ in a Suffering World*. Nashville: Abingdon, 2016.

Thurman, Howard. *Disciplines of the Spirit*. Richmond, IN: Friends United Press, 1963.

Timberg, Craig. "Russian propaganda may have been shared hundreds of millions of times, new research says." *The Washington Post* (October 5, 2017). https://www.washingtonpost.com/news/the-switch/wp/2017/10/05/russian-propaganda-may-have-been-shared-hundreds-of-millions-of-times-new-research-says/.

Tracy, Marc. "Howard cheerleaders add voices to the anthem debate by taking a knee." *The New York Times* (October 13, 2017). https://www.nytimes.com/2017/10/13/sports/ncaafootball/anthem-protests-howard-.html.

Truong, Debbie. "Fairfax County school district votes to rename J.E.B. Stuart High." *The Washington Post* (October 27, 2017). https://www.washingtonpost.com/local/education/fairfax-county-school-district-votes-to-rename-jeb-stuart-high/2017/10/27/b6ed43bc-119a-4fc3-b23d-fad22104181d_story.html.

Ura, Alexa. "Texas faith leaders come out against bills targeted at LGBT Texans." *The Texas Tribune* (May 3, 2017). https://www.texastribune.org/2017/05/03/texas-faith-leaders-come-out-against-bills-targeted-lgbt-texans/.

Van Dam, Andrew. "Is the GOP tax plan an unprecedented windfall for the wealthy? We look at 50 years of data to find out." *The Washington Post* (December 4, 2017). https://www.washingtonpost.com/news/wonk/wp/2017/12/04/is-the-gop-tax-plan-an-unprecedented-windfall-for-the-wealthy-we-look-at-50-years-of-data-to-find-out/?utm_term=.04d27e898a6d.

Waldman, Paul. "Why Trump's tax returns will keep causing Republicans headaches." *The Washington Post* (April 18, 2017). https://www.washingtonpost.com/blogs/plum-line/wp/2017/04/18/why-trumps-tax-returns-will-keep-causing-republicans-headaches/?utm_term=.621c12977d06.

Wang, Amy B. "Maxine Waters swings back at Bill O'Reilly: 'I'm a strong black woman and I cannot be intimidated.'" *The Washington Post* (March 29, 2017). https://www.washingtonpost.com/news/the-fix/wp/2017/03/28/bill-oreilly-compared-a-black-congresswomans-hair-to-a-james-brown-wig/?utm_term=.a30b7dfe6c82.

Bibliography

———. "Supreme Court upholds California's ban on gay 'conversion therapy." *The Washington Post* (May 2, 2017). https://www.washingtonpost.com/news/post-nation/wp/2017/04/27/lgbtq-people-were-born-perfect-a-new-bill-would-ban-conversion-therapy-nationwide/?utm_term=.25f7dc287b5b.

———. "Trump's science envoy quits in scathing letter with an embedded message: I-M-P-E-A-C-H." *The Washington Post* (August 23, 2017). https://www.washingtonpost.com/news/speaking-of-science/wp/2017/08/23/trumps-science-envoy-quits-with-scathing-letter-with-an-embedded-message-i-m-p-e-a-c-h/?utm_term=.75b624b70a00.

Washington Post Staff. "Washington Post's 2018 Pulitzer Prizes." *The Washington Post* (April 16, 2018). https://www.washingtonpost.com/news/national/wp/2018/04/16/feature/washington-post-wins-pulitzer-prizes-for-roy-moore-investigation-russia-reporting/?utm_term=.7434527bc6bb.

Weigel, David. "Who is Doug Jones, and can he defeat Roy Moore in conservative Alabama?" *The Washington Post* (September 27, 2017). https://www.washingtonpost.com/powerpost/who-is-doug-jones-and-can-he-defeat-roy-moore-in-conservative-alabama/2017/09/27/c89e2df2-a2fb-11e7-b14f-f41773cd5a14_story.html.

———. "Immigrant members of Congress ask Trump to keep DACA." *The Washington Post* (August 31, 2017). https://www.washingtonpost.com/news/powerpost/wp/2017/08/31/immigrant-members-of-congress-ask-trump-to-keep-daca/?noredirect=on.

Williams, Candace. "Trial dismissed against 'Homrich 9' water protestors." *The Detroit News* (June 21, 2017). https://www.detroitnews.com/story/news/local/detroit-city/2017/06/21/homrich-case-dismissed/103087798/.

Williams, Joseph. "Senate OKs 2 lawyers ABA says are 'not qualified." *U.S. News and World Report* (November 9, 2017). https://www.usnews.com/news/national-news/articles/2017-11-09/senate-recommends-for-lifetime-judgeships-two-lawyers-the-aba-deems-not-qualified.

Wines, Michael. "Asked for voters' data, states give Trump panel a bipartisan 'no." *The New York Times* (June 30, 2017). https://www.nytimes.com/2017/06/30/us/politics/kris-kobach-states-voter-fraud-data.html.

———. "Culling voter rolls: Battling over who even gets to go to the polls." *The New York Times* (November 25, 2017). https://www.nytimes.com/2017/11/25/us/voter-rolls-registration-culling-election.html.

Wong, Julia Carrie and Sam Levin. "Standing Rock Sioux: 'we can't back down now' on Dakota pipeline fight." *The Guardian* (January 25, 2017). https://www.theguardian.com/us-news/2017/jan/24/standing-rock-resistance-donald-trump-executive-order.

Yee, Vivian. "Judge blocks Trump effort to withhold money from sanctuary cities." *The New York Times* (April 25, 2107). https://www.nytimes.com/2017/04/25/us/judge-blocks-trump-sanctuary-cities.html.

———. "Judge temporarily halts new version of Trump's travel ban." *The New York Times* (October 17, 2017). https://www.nytimes.com/2017/10/17/us/trump-travel-ban-blocked.html.

Yeginsu, Ceylan. "What turned the British election? Maybe the youth vote." *The New York Times* (June 9, 2017). https://www.nytimes.com/2017/06/09/world/europe/britain-elections-youth-vote.html.

Bibliography

Zapotosky, Matt. "Justice Dept. compliance expert whose contract ended early says Trump conflicts made work feel hypocritical." *The Washington Post* (July 3, 2017). https://www.washingtonpost.com/world/national-security/justice-dept-compliance-expert-whose-contract-ended-early-says-trump-conflicts-made-work-feel-hypocritical/2017/07/03/c3d6b8e8-5ff8-11e7-a4f7-af34fc1d9d39_story.html.

Zuazmer, Julie. "Catholic nuns in Pa. build a chapel to block the path of a gas pipeline planned for their property." *The Washington Post* (July 16, 2017). https://www.washingtonpost.com/local/social-issues/catholic-nuns-in-pa-build-a-chapel-to-block-the-path-of-a-proposed-gas-pipeline/2017/07/16/0096e7ce-6a3c-11e7-96ab-5f38140b38cc_story.html.

Zuckerman, Jake. "Six arrested in Capito's office after day of protesting health care bill." *Charleston Gazette-Mail* (June 27, 2017). http://wvpress.org/breaking-news/six-arrested-capitos-office-day-protesting-health-care-bill/.

www.ingramcontent.com/pod-product-compliance
Lightning Source LLC
Chambersburg PA
CBHW022123160426
43197CB00009B/1139